FOR SALE

First published in 2012 by Carlton Books

Carlton Books Limited
20 Mortimer Street
London W1T 3JW

All rights reserved. No part of this publication
may be reproduced, stored in a retrieval
system, or transmitted in any form or by any
means, electronic, mechanical, photocopying,
recording, or otherwise, without prior
permission of the copyright owner and the
publishers.

ISBN: 978-1-78097-194-0

Project art editors: Darren Jordan
and Luke Griffin
Designer: Ben Ruocco
Production: Maria Petalidou
Words: Iain Spragg and Adrian Clarke
Project editor: Martin Corteel
Assistant editor: David Ballheimer

Printed and bound in Dubai

Right: *Mario Balotelli celebrates
after scoring his second goal
against Germany during their
Euro 2012 semi-final.*

Previous page: *A Guinea fan is
enjoying the football during the
Africa Cup of Nations.*

GARY LINEKER'S
FOOTBALL
It's Unbelievable!

SEEING THE FUNNY SIDE OF THE GAME

CARLTON
BOOKS

CONTENTS

Below upper left: *Wayne Rooney plays shadow puppeteer at Euro 2012.* **Below lower left:** *Sol Campbell is searched for a chest protector.* **Below middle:** *Paul Lambert proves he isn't that big-headed ... or the Champions League Trophy is that big.* **Below right:** *Referee Alan Robinson reacts to a penalty appeal from the visitors at Old Trafford.* **Opposite, clockwise from top left:** *Another Greek tragedy at Euro 2012 starring Giorgos Karagounis; Ian Wright tries to imitate Paul Gascoigne's Italia 90 tears; Fabien Barthez was pants in Men In Black 16; A naked pitch invader goes almost unnoticed and he's hopping mad about it; David James (right) can't cope with the strong wind and heavy matchball; the last fish Harry Redknapp caught was this long; Vinnie Jones treats the mascot like any opponent; Ronaldo knows just how much the bet was that he wouldn't play will in the World Cup with a silly haircut; Igor Stepanovs watches Ruud van Nistelrooy (right) try to head the beach ball blowing across the pitch at Euro 2004.*

INTRODUCTION

I was lucky enough to play football for 16 years and during my time as a professional, I travelled all over the world representing club and country. They were wonderful times and since I hung up my boots, I've been privileged to watch and discuss football for a living for the BBC on *Match of the Day*.

You might think that over the years I've seen pretty much everything the beautiful game has to offer. The truth is, I've hardly scratched the surface, and if I've learned anything from my experiences as both a player and presenter it's that when it comes to football, you really should expect the unexpected.

Football is essentially a simple game, so it's remarkable how often it still takes us all by surprise. Whether it's a breathtaking goal, an extraordinary match that rips up the rulebook, or a magical new trick from one of the game's great entertainers, football's ability to entertain and amaze is seemingly limitless.

Not that everything always goes exactly according to plan and for every perfectly executed free-kick or meticulously rehearsed set piece, there's a bungled back pass or terribly timed tackle that proves players and supporters alike really have no idea just what's going to happen next.

Goalkeepers, of course, are the prime suspects to suffer a cruel calamity at the worst possible time, apologetically picking the ball out of the back of the net after a moment of utter madness, but the 10 outfield players are far from immune to an embarrassing gaffe, and with the advent of the internet, their ridiculous misses, flagrant dives and hilarious mishaps can now be replayed online time and time again.

And as beautiful as football is, the players and managers don't always behave quite as impeccably as they should and whenever and wherever a ball is kicked, there are invariably outrageous examples of bad sportsmanship, temper tantrums and even full-scale brawls.

Football, however, isn't just weird and wonderful because of what happens on the pitch, and events on the 'other' side of the touchline often prove just as entertaining as the action in the middle with crazy supporters, extreme weather conditions, pitch invaders and madcap mascots just some of the entertaining examples of the game's extracurricular attractions.

The football circus, of course, doesn't just stop when the final whistle blows, and in the modern era, the lives of today's superstars off the pitch are scrutinised as closely as what they do during the game, with fans from all over the planet obsessed by the lifestyles of their heroes. And let's face it, there's no shortage of players who adore all the attention that is lavished upon them.

Football: It's Unbelievable! is a fitting title for an amazing collection of funny stories and amazing incidents about the game we all love, recounting countless mad moments and misadventures that prove even the game's greatest are susceptible to the occasional accident and meltdown.

It's also a book that casts an inquisitive eye around the wider world of football, from the far-flung corners of the globe to the village green, a journey that is as hilarious as it is informative. You'll be amazed by what you learn and by the time you've finished reading, you'll have enough anecdotes and trivia to impress even your most fanatical football friends.

Enjoy!

Gary Lineker, OBE

Below left to right: *Four shades of Gary: he can't bare to eat any other potato snack; "Hello sailor!"; showing off some violin tendencies; World Cup legend.*

CHAPTER 1

THE JOY OF FOOTBALL

The 90 dramatic and often manic minutes of a match are what players, managers and fans live for, and when the referee blows his whistle, nothing else matters. As a counter to wonder goals and amazing saves, things often don't go to plan and what happens next isn't what teams practise on the training ground all week. Whether it's an own goal or a gaffe, the red mist descending or an eye-watering injury, there are times when football makes complete fools out the very best of them. Sometimes the players have only themselves to blame for their embarrassment while other times they are victims of bad luck. Whatever the circumstances, the beautiful game definitely has a wicked sense of humour.

Didier Drogba rises highest to head a dramatic late equaliser for Chelsea against Bayern Munich in the 2012 Champions League final at the Allianz Arena.

Wonderful Wazza

Beating off some seriously stiff competition from numerous contenders, Wayne Rooney's sensational bicycle kick against Manchester City in 2011 was voted the greatest goal of the first 20 years of the Premier League. Manchester United's striker had bagged only four league goals in the previous seven months, but his audacious overhead effort – arrowed accurately into the top corner from 10 yards out – silenced his critics and proved that hanging in the air with your back to goal really is no excuse for not scoring.

WONDER GOALS

Goals can come in all shapes and guises but all supporters yearn to witness the wonder strike, the goal that dares to dazzle and take our breath away and as these examples prove, it's always worth the wait.

Magical Maradona

The 1986 World Cup quarter-final between Argentina and England may be infamous for Maradona's 'Hand of God' goal but to be fair to the midfielder, he did also score a sensational (and perfectly legal) second goal. Starting with a pirouette and burst of acceleration in his own half, the Argentinean maestro slalomed majestically through the statuesque England team before rounding Peter Shilton in goal. In 2000 it was named the 'Goal of the Century', although it remains a mystery how many (if any) disgruntled England supporters voted for the Argentinean's effort after his earlier skulduggery.

Brilliant Brazil

Before Spain's golden generation came along, Brazil's 1970 World Cup side were widely considered to be the best international team to have graced the planet and their fourth and final goal in the final against Italy typified their dazzling brilliance. The desperate Italians were chasing shadows but were finally put out of their misery when Pele languidly laid the ball off for Carlos Alberto, steaming down the right flank like a runaway train, to hit his shot without breaking stride. The ball rocketed into the far corner and what became known as 'the perfect goal' had just been scored.

Heads Up

Most wonder goals come from the boot but every now and then a player takes our breath away with a header. One of the best came from the forehead of England's Andy Carroll against Sweden during Euro 2012. Rising above the defence to meet a tantalising cross from Steven Gerrard, Carroll timed his leap to perfection and hit the ball with his considerable cranium with power and accuracy, spearing his header from 15 yards out past the goalkeeper. As England fans went wild Carroll was just glad his trademark ponytail hadn't got in the way.

Mario's Rocket

Sometimes the best goals come when they're least expected. That was the case when Italy beat Germany in the Euro 2012 semi-final thanks to a belter from Mario Balotelli. There seemed to be little danger when Riccardo Montolivo hit a hopeful pass forward, but Super Mario was first to react, bursting clear of the German defence and unleashing a sizzling shot from 18 yards out into the roof of the net.

HOW DID THEY MISS THAT?

Putting the ball in the back of the net is what most footballers dream of. Sadly, however, though that dream can often turn into a nightmare when a player has the goal firmly in their sights, only for them to suddenly panic and embarrassingly send the ball in completely the wrong direction.

The Iwelumo Incident

A classic example of missing a completely open goal, Scotland striker Chris Iwelumo was left scratching his head in disbelief when he failed to score against Norway at Hampden Park back in 2008. Team-mate Gary Naismith must have been pretty confused too after watching Iwelumo meet his inch-perfect cross just a metre in front of goal and then bizarrely side-foot the ball back towards him rather than past the stranded Norwegian keeper.

Torrid Torres

Fernando Torres cost Chelsea £50 million but the Blues definitely didn't get value for money when they faced Manchester United in 2011. To be fair, the Spanish striker did score in the game at Old Trafford but Torres still hit the headlines for all the wrong reasons when he took the ball past United goalkeeper David de Gea but then stuck out an awkward left foot and stabbed his shot wide of the post.

Keep It Simple

One of the golden rules of finishing is not to over-complicate things, which is exactly what Qatar's Fahad Khalfan didn't do in an Asian Games clash with Uzbekistan in 2010. Khalfan stole the ball after one of the Uzbekistan defenders panicked but as he raced towards the unguarded goal, the striker unwisely decided to showboat and hit the ball with the outside of his left boot. His effort kept curling, hit the post and bounced clear.

Second Time Unlucky

To miss one open goal can be considered unfortunate but to miss twice is just careless as Cesena's Emanuele Giaccherini embarrassingly discovered against Juventus in 2011. His first effort – a chip over the goalkeeper – hit the post but when the ball rolled invitingly back to him he failed to make the most of his good luck and hacked his shot high and wide. Bizarrely five months later Juventus decided Giaccherini's skills were just what they needed and signed him.

The Madness Of Mario

Some misses are the result of nerves. Some occur because of a cruel and untimely bobble of the ball. And then there are those that can be blamed squarely on the idiocy of the player, which was definitely the case when Mario Balotelli was on the pitch for Manchester City against LA Galaxy in their 2011 pre-season friendly in America. Clean through on goal, the Italian striker thought he'd be clever and pirouetted on the ball before trying to back heel the ball past the Galaxy keeper. The effort went wide while manager Roberto Mancini just went ballistic.

Villa The Villain

Spain won the World Cup in 2010 but star striker David Villa definitely wasn't on world-beating form a few months later when they faced Colombia in Madrid, hitting the post with the goal at his mercy and then slamming the rebound so wide that the ball actually went out for a throw-in. Luckily for Villa, he did find the back of the net five minutes from time to avoid a dressing down in the dressing room.

Crisis For Cristiano

Even the greatest players can have an unexplained horror show in front of goal, as Cristiano Ronaldo proved in 2006 playing for Manchester United against Sheffield United. Ryan Giggs dissected the Blades defence with a dazzling dribble, passed to an unmarked Ronaldo and then must have wondered why he bothered as the Portuguese casually chipped the ball harmlessly over the crossbar.

Water Hazard

Back passes can often have catastrophic consequences but sometimes it really isn't the players' fault and one such case was Sevilla's damp home clash with Almeria in 2010 when visiting captain Santiago Acasiete opted to pass to his goalkeeper. There seemed nothing wrong with the ball until it hit a puddle of water and stopped dead in its tracks, allowing midfielder Direni to steal in and set up Alvaro Negredo for the only goal of the game.

A Very Early Bath

A badly placed back pass at any time during a match is ill-advised but straight from the kick-off is simply suicidal, as Ebbsfleet United's Ryan Blake found out in 2011 during a league game against Farnborough when his limp early effort was intercepted by Kezie Ibe. The Farnborough striker raced towards goal only to be brought down in the area by goalkeeper Preston Edwards, who was unsurprisingly shown a red card by the referee after just 10 seconds.

Disaster For Dixon

Lee Dixon enjoyed a glittering career with Arsenal and England but the Gunners defender also dropped a few clangers during his 20 years in the professional game and his most incredible mistake came in 1991 when Arsenal faced Coventry at Highbury. The full-back received the ball 40 yards out from his own goal and with no options ahead of him, he decided to knock it back to goalkeeper David Seaman and start again. Unfortunately Dixon didn't bother to check where Seaman actually was and skilfully chipped his bemused team-mate with a curling but calamitous back pass.

BEWARE THE BACK PASS

Football is a game that really should be played going forward as a team strives to break down the opposition defence and score a glorious goal. Ignoring this golden rule by going in the other direction, passing the ball back to a blundering goalkeeper, is just asking for trouble.

Muddy Hell

Mud isn't the ideal playing surface but Crystal Palace striker Dougie Freedman definitely wasn't complaining after a patch of the sticky stuff helped him get on the score sheet against Sheffield Wednesday in 2002, latching onto an Ashley Westwood back pass that was 'delayed' by some brown sludge before firing past the goalkeeper.

The Danger Of Divots

Bumpy pitches are a nightmare for players at all levels of the beautiful game and even top-class internationals are wary of the dangers of an uneven surface. Just ask England goalkeeper Paul Robinson, who had to pick the ball out of his own net in a Euro 2008 qualifier against Croatia in Zagreb after Gary Neville's back pass hit a divot and bobbled over his swinging right boot.

Fabien Fails

Back passes are sometimes only as good as the goalkeeper on the receiving end of them and in the blink of an eye a careless custodian can turn a perfectly good ball into a disaster. A classic example came in 2001 when Manchester United's Fabien Barthez got a beautiful back pass from David Beckham but then inexplicably and under absolutely no pressure, hit his clearance straight to Arsenal's Thierry Henry on the edge of the box, who couldn't believe his luck and scored.

Achilles Heel

Spanish footballers are famous for their silky skills but they deserted defender Inigo Martinez while on Under-21 duty for his country in 2011 against Georgia. There seemed little danger when the Georgian keeper launched a hopeful long-range kick up the field but Martinez couldn't resist making an unconventional back pass, volleying the ball with an eye-catching back heel. Unfortunately, his effort ballooned off his boot, over his irate keeper and into the net from a full 40 yards out.

Head Boy

There isn't any rule that states a back 'pass' has to be made with the feet, which is why Real Madrid's Marcelo literally decided to use his head in 2010 against Real Zaragoza after goalkeeper Iker Casillas spilled a shot. As the ball rebounded out, Marcelo slid onto his chest and headed the ball back, snuffing out the danger but leaving the Madrid kit manager with the mother of all grass stains to deal with.

CELEBRATING IN STYLE

A good old-fashioned, simple handshake used to suffice when it came to celebrating a goal, but self-restraint has long since gone out of the window. Whether it's outrageous back flips, dynamic dance moves or the use of random comedy props, it seems some players simply can't contain their excitement when they hit the back of the net.

Diving German

Some people say Germans don't have a sense of humour but striker Jurgen Klinsmann certainly proved them wrong during his spells with Spurs in the 1990s, performing a spectacular 'splash dive' every time he scored to silence the critics who claimed he went down too easily under challenges. His first dive came after scoring on his debut on the opening day of the 1994–95 season, a 4–3 defeat of Sheffield Wednesday at Hillsborough. His Tottenham team-mates loved it too and half the team hit the deck chest first each time the German found the back of the net.

That's Pants

Some players simply can't resist the urge to undress when they score but Montenegro star Mirko Vucinic decided peeling off his shirt just wasn't enough in 2010 after finding the back of the net against Switzerland – whipping off his shorts, popping them onto his head and running around in his underwear like a crazed and slightly indecent lunatic.

Carrot Top

What do you do when you want to taunt your opponents who are nicknamed The Rabbits? According to Atletico Mineiro's Brazilian forward Edmilson Ferreira it's easy. You score a goal, pull a concealed carrot out of your shorts and start eating it like a bunny.

Fishing Fun

If trophies were awarded for clever goal celebrations, Icelandic top-flight side Stjarnan would win the Champions League. Stjarnan seem to spend all their spare time dreaming up elaborate new routines and the minnows have become YouTube sensations for creative masterpieces that include The Human Bicycle, Rambo and Giving Birth. Their pièce de résistance however came in 2010 after scoring against Fylkir when striker Halldor Orri caught Johan 'The Salmon' Laxdal on his imaginary fishing line and reeled him in, much to the amusement of millions of viewers online. Johan's realistic portrayal of the panic-stricken bouncing salmon was truly a sight to behold.

A Dog's Life

You can't always account for taste and there's no denying Nigerian striker Finidi George went barking mad after scoring a wonderful breakaway goal against Greece in the 1994 World Cup finals. Running towards the corner flag, nothing seemed untoward until the former Ajax star unexpectedly bent down onto all fours and crawled around like a dog before unexpectedly raising his back leg and pretending to urinate on the grass.

Mr Angry

Scoring a goal usually sparks an onset of unconfined joy but in Temuri Ketsbaia's case it turned him into a mad thing back in 1998. Frustrated at his lack of match action for Newcastle United, the Georgian international's last-minute winner at home to Bolton Wanderers prompted him to rip off his shirt, unceremoniously shove away his team-mates and literally boot the advertising hoardings behind the goal as hard as he possibly could three times.

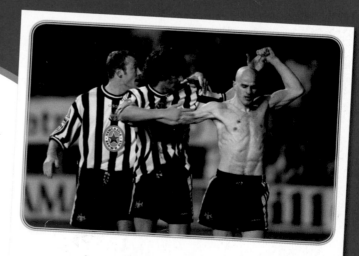

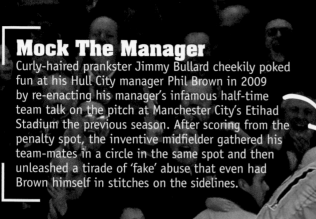

Mock The Manager

Curly-haired prankster Jimmy Bullard cheekily poked fun at his Hull City manager Phil Brown in 2009 by re-enacting his manager's infamous half-time team talk on the pitch at Manchester City's Etihad Stadium the previous season. After scoring from the penalty spot, the inventive midfielder gathered his team-mates in a circle in the same spot and then unleashed a tirade of 'fake' abuse that even had Brown himself in stitches on the sidelines.

Baby Bloomer

The sleepless nights and exhaustion that inevitably come with the arrival of a new baby can make parents do the strangest things. Chelsea's Frank Lampard joined the club in 2005 after scoring against West Brom, rocking an imaginary infant in his arms even though Lampard Junior was actually safely tucked up in bed at home. The routine had first been shown off by Brazil's Bebeto, celebrating the recent birth of his third child, after he had scored in the 1994 World Cup.

Cruel Finger Of Fate

One of the golden rules of football is that players must remove all items of jewellery before kick-off and if your wedding ring just won't come off, it's usually a good idea to tape over it. Just ask Paulo Diogo, who will forever regret not heeding this simple adage after an extremely painful goal celebration after scoring for Servette in 2004 against FC Schaffhausen in a Swiss League game. The midfielder leapt onto a metal perimeter fence to enjoy his moment of glory with the fans but didn't realise his wedding ring was caught in the metal, jumping down to resume the game and ripping his finger off in the process. To make matters even worse, the referee booked Diogo for 'excessive celebration' and despite the doctors' best efforts, his missing finger was never reattached.

Longest Celebration Ever

Sometimes a goal celebration can seem to go on. And on. And on. In the case of Rosario Central supporters in Argentina however, their commemoration of a goal scored by cult hero Aldo Poy is literally timeless. Back in 1971, Poy scored with a glorious diving header against arch rivals Newell's Old Boys to clinch the Argentinean title and every year since, Rosario fans from across the country have gathered together to party once again and remember Poy's fabled effort.

Tribute Act

Exactly how Brazilian Marcello Matrone ended up playing for Finnish Third Division outfit HIK remains a mystery but the forward obviously has too much time on his hands judging by his elaborate goal celebrations. Every time he scores, Matrone celebrates with a full-blown tribute performance to a famous rock star and the South American really hit the headlines in 2011 when he did a truly awful impression of Guns and Roses lead singer Axl Rose, donning a waist-length blonde wig and bandana and singing 'Sweet Child of Mine' into an upside-down mop that was masquerading as a microphone.

Kung Fu Fighting

It is far from unusual to run after your team-mate and give them a hearty slap on the back if they've just scored but it's altogether rarer to stand inside the six-yard box and start a fight with the opposition defenders. Yet that's exactly what happened when Herediano scored their fourth goal against Costa Rican league leaders Alajuelense in 2011. When the two sets of players had finally stopped kicking and punching the living daylights out of one another, the referee brandished a rather lenient four red cards.

Congolese Corker

Bouncing around on your bottom with both hands and feet in the air inside your penalty area like a deranged Duracell bunny takes some doing but Mazembe's goalkeeper Muteba Kidiaba made this rather peculiar art form look deceptively easy at the Club World Cup in 2010. Mazembe beat Brazil's Internacional to reach the final of the competition and Kidiaba decided to mark the occasion with an impromptu bout of bottom bouncing.

Going To The Dentist

The England squad that went on to lose in the Euro 96 semi-final, had received all sorts of bad publicity after it emerged they had played late-night drinking games in a dentist's chair during a tour of the Far East in the build-up to the tournament. Midfielder Paul Gascoigne however thought it was hilarious and after scoring a great solo goal against Scotland at Wembley, he hit the deck, lying on his back as if in a dentist's chair, and invited his team-mates to re-create the game by spraying water – rather than vodka – into his mouth. Steve McManaman, Alan Shearer and Jamie Redknapp were more than happy to oblige.

AMAZING SAVES

The life of the goalkeeper is not always a happy one with every mistake and misjudgement analysed and criticised in minute detail. But that's all forgotten in those rare moments when the game's custodians pull off truly spectacular saves.

Brilliant Banks

Pele was already preparing to celebrate as he watched his brilliant downward header fly towards the corner of Gordon Banks' net during the 1970 World Cup, but the Brazilian legend shouldn't have counted his chickens as the England goalkeeper scampered across the face of his goal, dived to his right and miraculously tipped the ball against and over the crossbar. It was a moment that defined Banks' career and his superhuman stop quickly became known as the 'save of the century'.

Johnson Denied

When the ball arrived at Glen Johnson's feet, just six yards from goal in England's Euro 2012 quarter-final against Italy, bookies would have said that the odds on the Liverpool defender scoring were very short indeed. But the bookmakers hadn't reckoned with *Azzurri* goalkeeper Gianluigi Buffon. He managed to get an outstretched left hand to Johnson's albeit mishit scoop shot and pawed the ball to safety. Johnson couldn't believe it. And neither, probably, could Buffon.

Safe Hands

Arsenal might have been the overwhelming favourites to beat Sheffield United in their 2003 FA Cup semi-final showdown but the Gunners ultimately owed their 1–0 win to one of the most sensational saves the game has seen when David Seaman contorted his body backwards to claw out a point-blank header from Blades striker Paul Peschisolido, a sensational stop that really had to be seen to be believed.

Hart Racing

It's always fun to see a goalkeeper go forward to try and score from a last-minute corner but it's even funnier watching him, manically racing back to his goal in a desperate bid to save a breakaway goal at the other end. Manchester City's Joe Hart did just this in 2010 when he was caught at the wrong end of the pitch but somehow still managed to get back in the nick of time and fist away Wayne Rooney's handsome 50-yard drive with the back of his gloves. City still lost the game 1–0 but Hart at least had won his own personal duel with Rooney.

Danish Defence

Peter Schmeichel used to terrify opposition strikers and his own defence in equal measure as he barked out his orders during his Manchester United days and the great Dane certainly had something to shout about in 1997 when he pulled off possibly the greatest save of his career to deny Liverpool's John Barnes, leaping like Superman across the face of goal to push away a far-post header from the winger that seemed destined to hit the back of the net.

World Cup Clanger

There's never a good time or place to let in a horror goal and England's Robert Green must surely have wished he hadn't left it until he was on the world's biggest stage – the 2010 World Cup – to produce his own moment of madness. With England leading 1–0 against the United States, Green seemed to have Clint Dempsey's hopeful, long-range effort comfortably covered but rather than cradle the weak shot into his chest like a new-born baby, the keeper let the ball slide off his gloves and roll apologetically into the net, gifting the Americans a 1–1 draw.

Costly Celebrations

Goalkeepers need to stay calm at all times, as proven by Hans Jorg Butt during a German league match in 2007. The Bayer Leverkusen star scored from the penalty spot to give his side a 3–1 lead but as he ran back, ecstatically high-fiving his team-mates and saluting the crowd, Schalke kicked off and Mike Hanke's strike sailed over the distracted custodian and into an unguarded net.

GOALKEEPER GAFFES

Playing in goal can be a thankless task and as every keeper knows, they can pull off a series of sensational saves only to be remembered for just one mistake, misjudgement or mishap.

On Your Head

Goalkeepers can be an absent-minded bunch and Bosnian Tomislav Piplica actually forgot goalkeepers are allowed to use their hands in a 2002 Bundesliga clash between FC Energie Cottbus and Borussia Moenchengladbach. Watching an opponent's volley deflect high into the air, his desperate team-mates screamed 'catch it' but the hapless custodian bizarrely allowed the ball to bounce off his head and into the goal.

Bad Acting

Play-acting is part of the modern day footballer's DNA but Chilean keeper Roberto 'Condor' Rojas took it to extremes in a crucial World Cup qualifying clash against Brazil in 1989. With Chile trailing in the second half, Rojas suddenly fell to the floor clutching his head claiming a firecracker thrown from the crowd had hit him. Blood was pouring from his head and the match was abandoned but after a review of the video footage, it emerged Rojas had cut his own head with a razor blade hidden in his gloves and had faked the whole thing. He never played again.

Holy Howler

It's all well and good asking for divine intervention during a match but you still have to keep your eye on the ball – which is exactly what Brazilian stopper Isadore Irandir didn't do when his Rio Preto side took on Corinthians in the early 1970s. Unaware that the match had already kicked off, the religious keeper was still on his knees praying to God as Roberto Rivelino's wondrous left-footed drive from the halfway line sailed into his empty net.

Two Left Feet

Plenty of keepers miskick bobbly back passes but a few simply trip over themselves, collapse in a heap and then watch the ball roll over their line. Stand up Virgil Vries, who earned himself internet notoriety in 2011 for achieving that very feat when playing for South African side Golden Arrows.

Taxi For Taibi

Goalkeeper Massimo Taibi cost Manchester United £4.5 million back in 1999 but he didn't exactly prove great value for money after producing one of the funniest gaffes in Premier League history. United were playing Southampton at Old Trafford when the butter-fingered Italian allowed Matt Le Tissier's scuffed shot from 25 yards out to go through his hands, under his body and between his legs for the softest goal imaginable. The following week he was part of the United side hammered 5–0 by Chelsea and he never played for the club again.

Higuita's Horror

Any goalkeeper who decides to have a dribble outside his area is just asking for trouble and that's exactly what Colombia's Rene Higuita, 'El Loco' (the Madman), got at the 1990 World Cup when he attempted an audacious Cruyff turn halfway up the pitch only to be dispossessed by Cameroon's Roger Milla. The African striker strolled gratefully towards the Colombia goal and despite Higuita's desperate two-footed lunge, Milla slotted home for one of the easiest goals of his long and famous career.

23

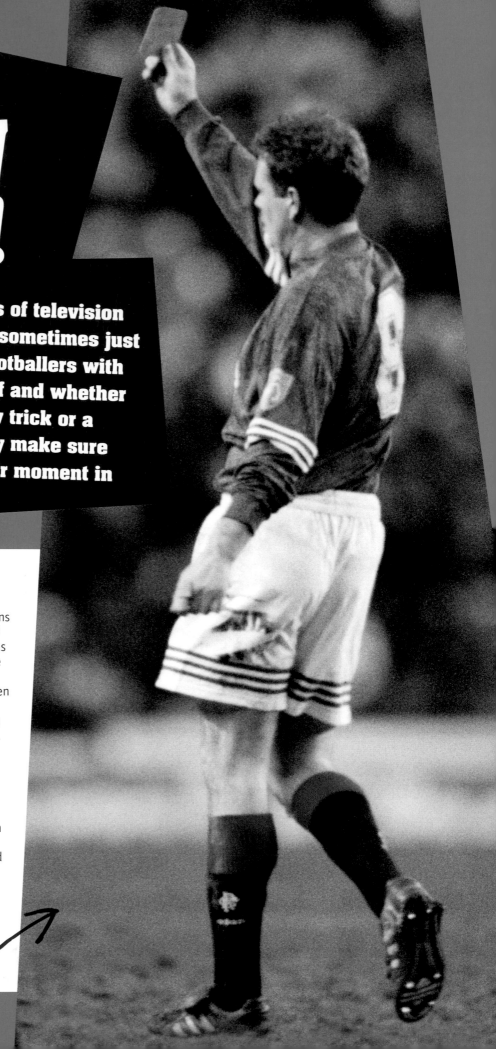

IT'S SHOW TIME!

Playing in front of millions of television viewers around the world sometimes just isn't enough for certain footballers with a penchant for showing off and whether it's with an audacious new trick or a cheeky joke, they certainly make sure they make the most of their moment in the spotlight.

Juggling Joker

Most of us have probably wondered what would happen if we started to juggle the ball in the middle of a game but Corinthians star Edilson actually tried it during a 1999 Cup final clash against arch rivals Palmeiras in Brazil. After a brief bout of keepy-uppie on the halfway line, the striker rolled the ball down the back of his neck but was then booted unceremoniously into the air by several angry Palmeiras players, sparking a 22-man brawl. The match was abandoned and Edilson was dropped by Brazil for causing the riot.

Card Games

When butter-fingered referee Dougie Smith dropped his notebook during a Scottish Premier League clash between Rangers and Hibs in 1995, Paul Gascoigne noticed the careless official had left his yellow card on the Ibrox turf. The midfield prankster promptly brandished the card in Smith's direction much to the amusement of the crowd but the grumpy referee failed to see the joke, grabbed his card back and booked Gascoigne for his impudence.

Seal Of Disapproval

Showboating can sometimes be a painful business, as Brazilian midfielder Kerlon discovered in 2007 when he decided to try out his 'seal dribble' in a game for Cruzeiro against Atletico Madrid, flicking the ball up and running past the opposition as he repeatedly bounced it on his forehead. Unfortunately Atletico's Diego Rocha was not amused and brought Kerlon's antics to an abrupt end with a hefty forearm smash. Rocha got a red card and a 120-day ban for the attack while Kerlon got a very sore jaw.

Beer Shower

It takes courage (or perhaps downright stupidity) for anyone to tip a pint of beer over the head of their boss, but that didn't seem to worry over-excited Olcay Sahan when he began the celebrations after Duisberg's DFB Cup semi-final win over Energie Cottbus in 2011. Judging by the look on Milan Sasic's face, he certainly wasn't expecting to be showered in booze, but at least he was wearing a tracksuit rather than an expensive and immaculately tailored suit favoured by some managers in Germany.

Funny Face

Different players react to hostile crowds in different ways. In 1985, when Liverpool travelled to Old Trafford for an always tense league match, madcap Liverpool goalkeeper Bruce Grobbelaar decided to have a laugh with the naughty Manchester United fans who had been throwing coins onto the pitch during the game. He bent down, picked up the cash and popped the coins onto his eyes, before pulling the kind of face that probably gave some of the younger supporters on the terraces a few sleepless nights.

Bum Note

Players ripping off their shirt after scoring a goal has become a common sight in football, even though they will be shown a yellow card, but Arsenal's defender Sammy Nelson decided to go with an altogether cheekier celebration after finding the back of the net against Coventry in April 1979. He charged towards the fans standing at the North Bank end of Highbury, lowered his shorts and exposed his bottom. The supporters found it hilarious but Nelson wasn't laughing when Arsenal fined him two weeks' wages for his ill-advised moon.

NUTMEGS AND TRICKS

Naughty nutmegs and tremendous tricks can light up even the most boring of matches and even though you won't often find them in the coaching manuals, they are skills which supporters all over the world just can't get enough of.

Eder's Artistry
Losing 4–0 in a World Cup finals game is bad enough but Brazil's Eder decided to add insult to injury against poor old New Zealand in Spain in 1982 when he nutmegged Glenn Dods, no doubt leaving the embarrassed Kiwi wishing that he'd taken up rugby rather than football like the majority of his compatriots.

Mexican Magic
Football's answer to the kangaroo, the maverick Mexican winger Cuauhtemoc Blanco lit up the 1998 World Cup finals with a sparkling move called, you've guessed it, 'The Blanco'. Faced by opposition players, the cheeky wide man would wedge the ball between his feet, leap between his open-mouthed opponents and then release the sacred sphere before hitting the ground and sprinting clear.

The Flying Flick
The volley is one of football's toughest skills to master but it's even more difficult when you try to hit one with a flying back heel. Many have tried and failed to execute this outrageous trick but Metalist Kharkiv midfielder Cleiton Xavier pulled it off in a game against Dnipro in 2011, flicking a cross into the back of his net with a stunning mid-air touch from behind his back.

Rooney's Shame
When Nike were filming a TV advert in 2009, the star of the show was meant to be Wayne Rooney but it was actually a 19-year-old by the name of Callam Roberts who grabbed the glory, nutmegging the England star during a five-a-side game and almost ruining the striker's reputation overnight.

Breaking The Rules
Most goalkeepers don't relish taking unnecessary risks but former Manchester United stopper Fabien Barthez wasn't one of them and back at Old Trafford in 2001 he lived the dream when he nutmegged an outfield player. The unlucky chap was Derby County's Lee Morris, who stood aghast as the Frenchman rolled the ball between his legs when he really should have done the decent thing and thrashed it up field.

Thierry's Tricks

Houdini was famous for escaping from seemingly impossible situations but even he might have learned a thing or two from a fantastic bit of skill by Arsenal's Thierry Henry in 2004. He nutmegged Middlesbrough's Danny Mills by the flag and danced past the bemused defender who probably thought he had him safely trapped in the corner.

The Scorpion

When a goalkeeper earns the nickname 'The Madman', it's safe to assume he'll be entertaining and custodian Rene Higuita certainly lived up to his billing in 1995 when Colombia played England at Wembley with an unbelievable 'scorpion kick'. England's Jamie Redknapp looped a harmless-looking shot towards the goal but rather than taking the safe option of actually catching the ball, Higuita leapt forwards and cleared the danger in mid-air with the heels of both boots.

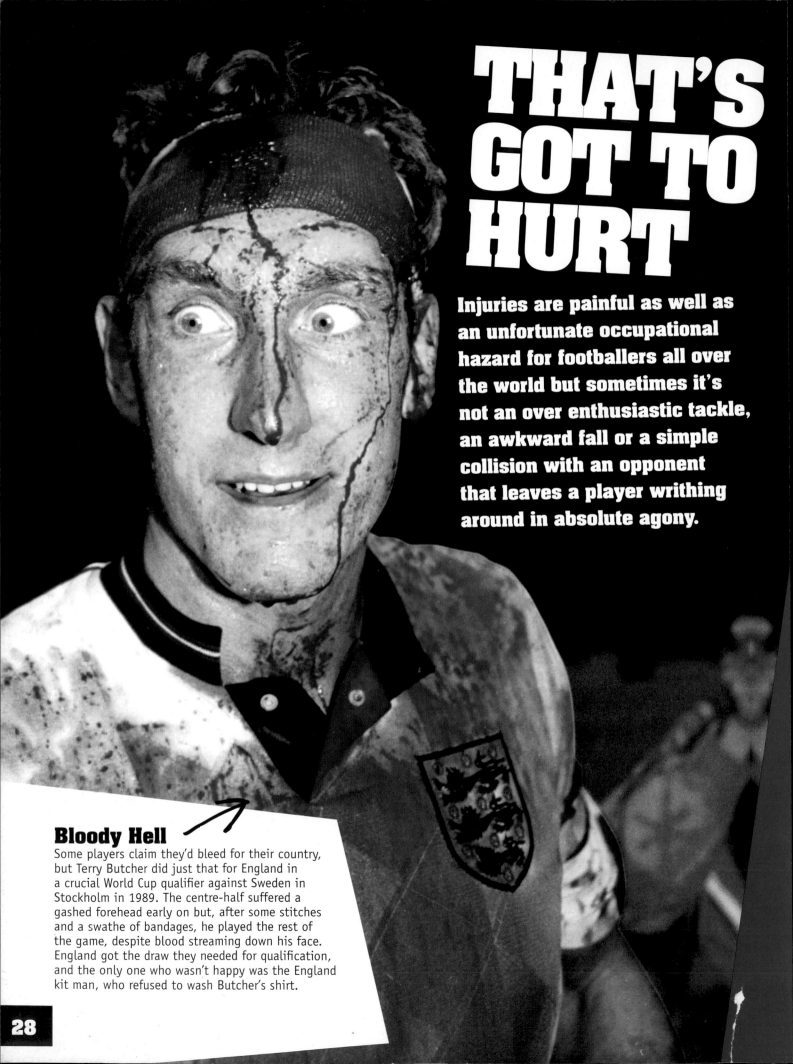

THAT'S GOT TO HURT

Injuries are painful as well as an unfortunate occupational hazard for footballers all over the world but sometimes it's not an over enthusiastic tackle, an awkward fall or a simple collision with an opponent that leaves a player writhing around in absolute agony.

Bloody Hell

Some players claim they'd bleed for their country, but Terry Butcher did just that for England in a crucial World Cup qualifier against Sweden in Stockholm in 1989. The centre-half suffered a gashed forehead early on but, after some stitches and a swathe of bandages, he played the rest of the game, despite blood streaming down his face. England got the draw they needed for qualification, and the only one who wasn't happy was the England kit man, who refused to wash Butcher's shirt.

Babb Busted

Defenders just hate conceding goals and Liverpool centre-half Phil Babb certainly went to eye-watering extremes to stop Chelsea scoring in a Premier League clash at Anfield back in 1998 when striker Pierluigi Casiraghi went round goalkeeper David James and slid the ball towards goal. Babb slide desperately across the grass to intercept but with his legs spread, he couldn't stop himself as the post loomed and smacked into the woodwork groin first. The doctor rushed on while every male supporter in the ground winced in sympathy.

Savage Blow

Danger can lurk in the most unlikely of places on a football pitch and Leicester City's Robbie Savage certainly wasn't expecting to be poleaxed by referee Matt Messias during his side's 1993 clash with Newcastle. Messias flung his arm out to indicate a foul but had no idea the Foxes star was jogging up behind him and smashed the unlucky midfielder square in the face with his right elbow. Savage was probably not amused as he slumped to the floor but Newcastle's Alan Shearer thought it was hilarious, showing Messias his own red card for the unprovoked attack.

Massive Michael

Striker Michael Ricketts, who earned one full England cap, was what is known as a 'big unit' and the six-foot-three forward certainly made his impressive physique count when he had an accidental collision with a linesman during Tranmere Rovers' 2009–10 campaign. Told to warm up by his manager, Ricketts was trotting innocently up and down the touchline when he crashed into the unsuspecting assistant referee and although the striker barely noticed the bump, the linesman was knocked out cold and needed emergency medical attention.

Foot And Mouth

Gumshields are usually associated with the ugly free-for-all that is rugby, but Dutch defender Demy de Zeeuw probably wished he'd invested in a spot of dental protection after Uruguay's Martin Caceres horribly mistook his head for the ball during the 2010 World Cup semi-final in Cape Town.

Danns Undamaged

Staying on your feet is usually a good idea for strikers as they search for that all-important goal, but Crystal Palace's Neil Danns certainly failed to heed that advice. Playing against Barnsley at Selhurst Park in April 2011, he clattered into advertising hoardings, flipped over them, almost took out a photographer and went face first into the concrete. Amazingly, he got up immediately and, seconds later, returned to the action.

Eyesore

A pre-match warm-up is designed to guard against injuries but things didn't exactly go according to plan before Bayern Munich's Bundesliga game against Arminia Bielefeld in 2006 when Michael Rensing hit a powerful shot at Oliver Khan. The Bayern Munich goalkeeper made a complete mess of stopping Rensing's vicious strike and the ball smacked straight into his face, leaving the German international with an enormous black eye that forced him to sit out the match.

Girly Grappling

If you're a cynical and downright dirty defender, the sight of a ponytailed centre-forward is probably just too much to resist. University of New Mexico defender Elizabeth Lambert proved the point during a Mountain West Conference semi-final in 2009 when she got a glimpse of the Brigham Young University striker Kassidy Shumway. Not content with viciously yanking the forward's hair while the referee wasn't looking, naughty Lambert also landed a vicious short-armed punch into Carlee Payne's back, also well away from play. Justice was done however when she received a two-match ban after officials reviewed the video evidence.

SPOT THE BALL

Football is a game that's played with a spherical object commonly known as 'the ball'. But don't be fooled into following the ball at all times because plenty of interesting and frequently nasty things happen when it's nowhere in sight.

On Me Back Son!

Centre-half Rio Ferdinand and Carlos Tevez were Manchester United team-mates before the Argentinean striker signed for rivals Manchester City in July 2009. When the two teams met at Old Trafford the following year, the old pals obviously decided to get 'reacquainted'. The expression on Ferdinand's face suggests he didn't enjoy the reunion quite as much as snood-wearing Tevez, whose claim he was only playing 'Spot the ball' wasn't believed.

Timely Trip

Not all off-the-ball incidents are worthy of a place in the game's Hall of Shame as Adrian Jesus Bastia proved during a Greek Super League clash between Panathinaikos and Asteras Tripolis in 2008. Enraged by Panathinaikos' poor performance, one rebellious fan ran onto the pitch in protest and was duly chased by a less-than-athletic bunch of local riot police who were struggling to keep up. Doing his good deed for the day, Asteras' Argentinean midfielder Bastia cleverly tripped the invader so that he could finally be apprehended. He was rewarded for his quick thinking with a red card by the referee and an early bath.

Mayor Mayhem

Charity matches are meant to be friendly affairs but Mayor of London Boris Johnson spectacularly ignored such protocol during an England versus Germany Legends game in 2006. Much to the amusement of the 15,000 fans inside Reading's Madejski Stadium, mop-haired Boris charged like a rampant bull towards Germany's Maurizio Gaudino and stumbled head first into his opponent's groin, flattening him in the process. The ball was nowhere to be seen at the time, an irony not lost on the wincing Gaudino.

Human Punchbag

It's not unknown for players to goad an opponent into taking a swing at them in the hope that they'll get sent off while other devious footballers are more than happy to invite a head butt or even a kick to the shins if it means they'll gain a numerical advantage during a match. Chilean Under-21 player Bryan Carrasco however took this approach to a whole new level in 2011 against Ecuador when he grabbed an opponent's arm and then 'punched himself' in the face with their fist.

Hollywood Hooligan

Before becoming a movie star, Vinnie Jones spent most of his time in the Wimbledon midfield scaring the wits out of anyone stupid or brave enough to come anywhere near him and back in February 1988 during a match at home to Newcastle United, Paul Gascoigne made the foolhardy decision to mark vicious Vinnie at a free-kick. In an instant the would-be actor stepped back onto Gazza's toes, reached behind him and promptly grabbed the terrified teenager's 'crown jewels'.

Bottoms Up

Spanish hardmen didn't come any tougher or more volatile that Sevilla centre-half Pablo Alfaro, a player who was willing to do almost anything to win all three points for his team. Aside from being remembered for a whole host of terrible tackles, the dirty defender is perhaps best known for shoving his hand up the bottom of a rather shocked Atletico Madrid front man during a 2004 Copa del Rey clash. Now that's what you call extremely tight man-to-man marking.

Short Shrift

The 2011 clash between Olympiakos and AEK Athens featured a great moment of comedy when defender Francois Modesto took revenge for a tackle from AEK player Cala, pulling down his opponent's shorts to reveal a pair of fetching white Y-fronts.

LOSING THE PLOT

Football has an uncanny knack of getting so many people all hot and bothered and whether it is the game's players, managers, match officials or the supporters, moments of madness in the heat of battle really aren't all that unusual.

Pushing Your Luck

Fits of temper came as naturally as scoring goals to former Premier League star Paolo di Canio and his infamous meltdown for Sheffield Wednesday against Arsenal in 1998 is now the stuff of legend. Not prepared to accept the red card referee Paul Alcock had shown him, the angry Italian reacted by shoving him in the chest, causing quite possibly the most comical stumble and fall that football has ever seen. Resembling someone who'd just sunk 15 pints of lager Alcock wobbled, staggered and eventually fell backwards on to the turf while Di Canio was handed an 11-match ban for his crime.

Eric Enraged

French legend Eric Cantona was never far from the headlines during his controversial career and he racked up another blemish on his colourful CV in 1994 when Manchester United faced Leeds United in the FA Cup, poking Steve Hodge in the nose during a fiery clash at Old Trafford before running to the bench to ask if he could borrow a hanky.

Feeble Fight

If proof were ever needed that footballers are a bunch of softies, Sevilla's Luis Fabiano and Real Zaragoza's Carlos Diogo provided ample evidence in 2007 with the most embarrassing 'punch-up' ever witnessed in La Liga. After going nose-to-nose, the pathetic pair embarked on a hilarious bout of powder-puff punching that saw no one come remotely close to landing a meaningful blow. When he managed to stop laughing, the referee booked the pair of them.

Red Mist Of Zidane

Perhaps the most infamous (and stupid) red card in football history was when France's Zinedine Zidane got his marching orders in extra-time of the 2010 World Cup final following his headbutt into the chest of Italy's Marco Materazzi. With the ball miles away, the fiery playmaker, in his final game before retiring, couldn't even claim he had mistimed a header. As he enjoyed his early soak in the bath, France were losing to the Italians in a penalty shoot-out.

Everyone Off

South American football is no stranger to mass brawls but the 2011 Argentinean Fifth Division clash between Claypole and Victoriano broke new ground when referee Damian Rubino sent off a world record 36 players, substitutes and coaching staff after an ugly pitch battle between the two clubs broke out in the second half.

Getting Shirty

If you're going to foul a player, you've got to be prepared to face the consequences and Leeds' Billy Bremner suddenly realised he'd hacked down the wrong man in 1966 when Spurs enforcer Dave Mackay grabbed him by the collar after his fellow Scot's tasty tackle. The 'innocent face' fooled no one, but Bremner – no angel himself – saw he'd bitten off more than he could chew and steered clear of the Tottenham skipper for the rest of the match.

Magpies Melee

Team-mates are meant to exchange passes rather than punches but that's just what happened when Newcastle United pair Kieron Dyer and Lee Bowyer came to blows during a home defeat to Aston Villa in 2009. Losing 3–0 at the time and already down to ten men, the Magpie midfielders suddenly went for each other in front of 50,000 stunned fans at St James' Park and both collected a red card for their trouble.

JUST ABOUT THE PLAYERS

Without the 22 players out on the pitch (and the poor, frustrated souls who spend most matches warming the bench), the beautiful game would not be nearly as attractive and we'd all eventually have to find different ways to spend our Saturday afternoons. Footballers, however, come in many shapes and sizes, and for every shy and retiring model professional there is invariably a tortured extrovert who prefers to stand out from the crowd and dare to look just that little different. This chapter pays tribute to the players everywhere who don't follow the rules, the ones who provide almost as much entertainment off the pitch as they do on the hallowed turf, proving that football is a game which welcomes some of weirdest and most wonderful characters out there.

Mario Balotelli is prevented from speaking his mind, after coming off the bench to score Italy's decisive goal against the Republic of Ireland at Euro 2012.

CHAPTER 2

Daft David

There was nothing at all unusual about David Icke's brief career as a goalkeeper with Coventry and Hereford United but what happened next was truly remarkable. Forced to retire through arthritis at the age of 21, Icke initially forged a career as a TV sports presenter but then went spectacularly off the rails when he became interested in New Age philosophies and in 1991 he publicly predicted the world would end in six years' time. He later declared himself the son of God before saying the Earth was secretly ruled by a race of reptile-like aliens but it was his claim that Accrington Stanley would be crowned Premier League champions by 2015 which convinced everyone he'd really lost the plot.

Geography Lesson

Nicknamed 'Drillo', Norwegian Egil Olsen has never been a typical manager and although Wimbledon fans will never forget his penchant for wearing Wellington boots on the touchline, his unusual choice of footwear was merely the tip of the iceberg. A member of the Norwegian Workers' Communist Party, Olsen was also famed for memorising the height of every mountain on the planet and was so obsessed with geographical trivia that he wrote a 2002 book entitled *Drillo's World*, which sadly failed to trouble the Norwegian top 10 best sellers list.

Enigmatic Eric

Arguably the godfather of the game's genuine mavericks, Eric Cantona's eccentricity extended far beyond his trademark upturned collar. Punching team-mates, throwing the ball at referees and calling members of the French FA idiots all marked him out as 'different' early in his career but his infamous kung-fu kick at a Crystal Palace fan in 1995 while at Manchester United was probably his pièce de résistance. The temperamental Frenchman then hit the headlines when he famously said "when the seagulls follow the trawler, it's because they think sardines will be thrown into the sea" in a press conference called after he was convicted in court and he has continued to impress and confuse in equal measure as an actor since hanging up his boots.

Animal Magic

Plenty of players are superstitious but Fulham's Senegalese midfielder Papa Bouba Diop took it to a new level in 2004. The Cottagers were hovering nervously above the relegation places so Diop decided to perform a traditional 'ju-ju' ritual (a kind of West African voodoo) at Craven Cottage to change the team's luck, sprinkling animal blood over the pitch. The groundsman was furious but the magical intervention seemed to work and Fulham finished the season safely in 13th place.

THINKING OUTSIDE THE BOX

Some footballers are perfectly sane and rational people who quietly go about their business without hitting the headlines. Others however enjoy being that little bit different, as this weird and wonderful collection of the game's eccentrics goes to prove.

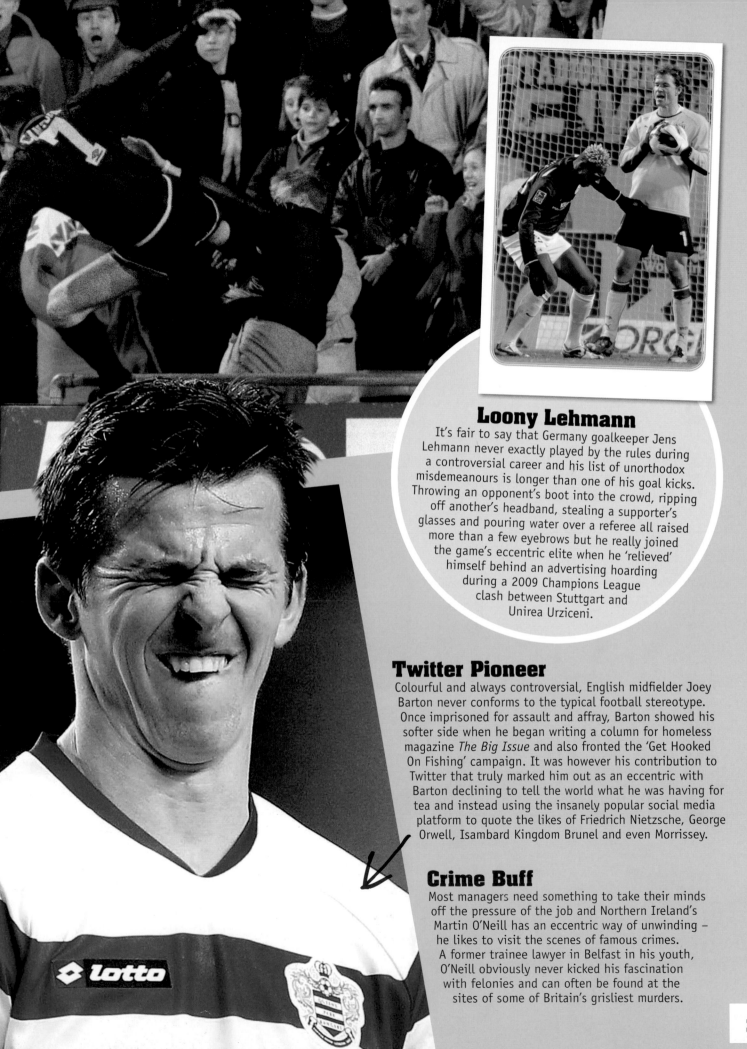

Loony Lehmann

It's fair to say that Germany goalkeeper Jens Lehmann never exactly played by the rules during a controversial career and his list of unorthodox misdemeanours is longer than one of his goal kicks. Throwing an opponent's boot into the crowd, ripping off another's headband, stealing a supporter's glasses and pouring water over a referee all raised more than a few eyebrows but he really joined the game's eccentric elite when he 'relieved' himself behind an advertising hoarding during a 2009 Champions League clash between Stuttgart and Unirea Urziceni.

Twitter Pioneer

Colourful and always controversial, English midfielder Joey Barton never conforms to the typical football stereotype. Once imprisoned for assault and affray, Barton showed his softer side when he began writing a column for homeless magazine *The Big Issue* and also fronted the 'Get Hooked On Fishing' campaign. It was however his contribution to Twitter that truly marked him out as an eccentric with Barton declining to tell the world what he was having for tea and instead using the insanely popular social media platform to quote the likes of Friedrich Nietzsche, George Orwell, Isambard Kingdom Brunel and even Morrissey.

Crime Buff

Most managers need something to take their minds off the pressure of the job and Northern Ireland's Martin O'Neill has an eccentric way of unwinding – he likes to visit the scenes of famous crimes. A former trainee lawyer in Belfast in his youth, O'Neill obviously never kicked his fascination with felonies and can often be found at the sites of some of Britain's grisliest murders.

It Started With A Kiss

Just why Fabien Barthez allowed it to happen remains a mystery but during the 1998 World Cup, France skipper Laurent Blanc got into the unusual habit of kissing his goalkeeper's bald head before kick-off. And it wasn't just a quick peck either, with Blanc grabbing his team-mate and giving him a long, lingering smooch before every match. It worked wonders though and France went on to be crowned world champions.

Gut Feeling

In order to psyche himself up, Dutch legend Johann Cruyff insisted on slapping Ajax keeper Gert Bals as hard as he could across the stomach before each match. Cruyff also spat his chewing gum into the opposition's half seconds before kick-off and the one time he forgot his gum, Ajax lost 4–1 to AC Milan in the final of the 1969 European Cup.

Spitting Mad

Former England goalkeeper David James couldn't truly get his game face on until every player had finished using the urinals prior to kick-off and once his team-mates had all relieved themselves, James popped into the toilets and bizarrely spat phlegm straight at the nearest wall.

PRE-MATCH RITUALS

Psyching themselves up for 90 minutes of action can certainly make footballers do the funniest things and whether it's at home, on the way to the match or inside the stadium itself, it's amazing just what goes on before that first whistle blows.

Malvin's Movie

Many footballers get nervous prior to kick-off but nobody dealt with those apprehensions in quite the same way as former Cardiff City and Huddersfield Town winger Malvin Kamara, who made sure he watched *Willy Wonka and the Chocolate Factory* before every single appearance. Kamara though obviously wasn't a Johnny Depp fan and insisted on watching the 1971 original of Roald Dahl's classic starring Gene Wilder rather than the 2005 remake.

Culture Vulture

Italian football has seen plenty of hard men over the years and Gennaro Gattuso continued that fine tradition with AC Milan by picking fights with a seemingly endless stream of opponents. In the dressing room, however, Gattuso is an altogether more intellectual rather than physical type of chap and prepares himself for the heat of battle – and inevitable punch-up – by immersing himself in the highbrow works of Russian novelist Fyodor Dostoyevsky while sat on the toilet. Whether his favourite Dostoyevsky work is *The Idiot* is unclear.

The Madness Of Mascorro

To describe Mexican defender Oscar Mascorro's pre-match build-up as meticulous would be an understatement. To call it obsessive however would be spot on. Mascorro begins a matchday by getting out of bed on the right side and making sure his right foot always touches the ground first. His pre-match meal is always hamburger, vanilla milkshake and apple juice and once inside the dressing room, he applies bandages to both wrists and scribbles down the letters M & P (the Spanish for mother and father), his own name and his girlfriend's surname on them. Once finally out on the pitch, he digs up a piece of turf and prays for good luck before collapsing with nervous exhaustion.

Tanked Up

Most pre-match rituals take place inside the sanctuary of the stadium but Spanish international Pepe Reina psyches himself up at his local BP garage on Merseyside, proving goalkeepers really are mad by refusing to play for Liverpool unless his petrol tank is full to the brim before kick-off.

Barmy Barber

Everyone knows that goalkeepers are a strange breed and Peterborough's Fred Barber merely confirmed everyone's suspicions when he emerged from the dressing room for the 1992 Division Three Play-Off Final against Stockport wearing a bizarre 'old man' mask. After a doctor reluctantly confirmed Barber wasn't actually clinically insane, the referee ordered the crazy keeper to remove the mask and Peterborough went on to win the match 2–1.

Musical Confession

When you love playing football as much as the ever excitable Wayne Rooney, calming down before kick-off rather than getting motivated is the problem and Wazza's novel if embarrassing solution is to don his headphones and listen to Scottish crooner Susan Boyle. "Her voice is amazing," said Rooney. "It relaxes me before a game."

BEFORE THEY WERE FAMOUS

Everyone knows that modern footballers earn a fortune these days but before turning professional and picking up their huge pay cheques, plenty of players came from far more modest (and less wealthy) backgrounds.

Fists Of Fury

Born in the Croxteth suburb of Liverpool in 1985, Wayne Rooney spent most of his childhood with a football at his feet but the future England star still found time to pull on a pair of gloves and do boxing training at his local gym. By all accounts, Wazza was a decent fighter but he had to pack in the pugilism at the age of 15 when his first club Everton told him to concentrate on scoring goals rather than walloping people, advice which he has occasionally forgotten during his subsequent football career.

Petrol Phil

A legend in South American football, Luis Felipe 'Big Phil' Scolari lifted the 2002 World Cup as Brazil manager but back in the 1960s he was a struggling semi-professional player and to supplement his modest wages he used to work as a part-time petrol pump attendant in the town of Porto Alegre.

Glass Cash

David Beckham is a multi-millionaire thanks to his wages from football, various endorsement deals and, of course, his own range of Y-fronts but before joining Manchester United as a teenager the England star earned a crust as a pot boy at his local greyhound track. "I always remember my time working at Walthamstow dogs," he said. "I picked up glasses at the track. It was my first job and I was so happy to be getting a wage for the first time."

Little Lionel

The greatest footballer on the planet, Lionel Messi was so tiny as a child in Argentina that doctors told him he needed growth hormone treatment if he was going to grow big enough to play professionally. His club River Plate could not afford to pay for the necessary drugs, so Spain's Barcelona offered to foot the medical bill. The rest, as they say, is history.

Diego's Skills

Raised in a shantytown on the outskirts of Buenos Aires in Argentina, Diego Maradona got his first break with a team called 'The Little Onions' but it was when he became a ball boy for Argentinos Juniors that his career took off, entertaining the crowds at half-time with his amazing ball-juggling skills.

Paper Trail

Beanpole England striker Peter Crouch has featured on plenty of newspaper back pages but growing up, the six-foot-seven forward briefly used to stoop down to local letterboxes to deliver them for a living. "I did a paper round as a kid but the early mornings were too much," he admitted. "My dad took it over, so I was getting paid £15 a week but he was doing it."

Criminal Proceeds

Birmingham City paid Southend £800,000 to lure Ricky Otto to St Andrews in 1994, making the striker the club's record signing at the time. Otto however had a chequered past before his football career and served four years for armed robbery as a teenager.

Rubbish Work

German midfielder Michael Ballack made his name at Kaiserslautern, Bayer Leverkusen, Bayern Munich and Chelsea but before signing his first professional contract with minnows Chemnitzer FC in the 1990s, he used to roam the streets of his hometown of Görlitz looking for rubbish. "When I was a kid, I used to collect wastepaper and bottles," Ballack explained. "The wastepaper earned me quite a lot of money. I'd take off every two or three weeks and pick up everything I could find."

Holy Orders

Some footballers pray before a game in the hope of a good result but Gavin Peacock began offering up his prayers after retiring in 2001. The midfielder initially followed a familiar path for countless ex-players and pursued a career in the media, appearing on the BBC's prestigious *Match of the Day*, but the devout former Newcastle and Chelsea star soon found himself listening to a higher calling and in 2008 he emigrated to Canada to train to be a priest.

On Song

Plenty of footballers enjoy a spot of karaoke after a hard match but former Northern Ireland midfielder Jim Whitley was so good at belting out a tune that he became a professional singer once his legs waved the white flag, playing the part of legendary American Sammy Davis Junior in a touring production of *The Rat Pack's Back* as well as appearing as Nat 'King' Cole in a show called *Christmas Crooners*.

The Chivers Inn

Martin Chivers was a star turn for Spurs in the late 1960s and 1970s but the forward went from White Hart Lane legend to landlord after playing his last game as a professional, pulling pints rather than his hamstring in a hotel and bar in Hertfordshire. Many players from that era took over pubs, but ex-Manchester City and England striker Francis Lee provided a better service – he ran a multi-million-pound toilet paper-making company.

WHAT THEY DID NEXT

Many players stay in football when the advancing years and their tired legs finally force them hang up their boots, educating the next generation as coach or manager. Others however turn their back on the beautiful game altogether to pursue very different alternative careers.

Making An Exhibition

Footballers do not exactly enjoy a reputation as culture vultures but French legend Lillian Thuram bucked the trend after his 18 years in the game when he curated an exhibition at the Quai Branly Museum in Paris. The exhibition was called 'Human Zoos: Invention of the Savage' and had absolutely nothing whatsoever to do with the beautiful game.

A Serious Undertaking

England's victory over West Germany in the 1966 World Cup final was an iconic moment which the nation celebrated for days but winner Ray Wilson chose a much more sombre occupation in retirement. He set up a funeral parlour in Huddersfield.

Book Worm

A serious knee injury forced Jack Ross to stop playing in 2011 but the Scottish defender was determined not to let his 16 years of experience with Falkirk, St Mirren and Dunfermline go to waste, dusting off his laptop to write a series of children's football books. The first in the series was called *Alfie the Adventurous Winger* with new titles *Danny the Determined Defender* and *Calum the Courageous Keeper* set to follow.

Flash Fash

John Fashanu was a charismatic player for Norwich, Aston Villa and Wimbledon but since he last kicked a ball in anger, the striker has embarked on a successful career as a TV personality, fronting *Gladiators* before landing the job as the host of the Nigerian version of *Deal or No Deal* back in 2007.

WORST KITS

Some shirts are so stylish and fashionable that supporters can wear their replica kit with real pride. Some, however, are just so painful on the eye that not even the most loyal fan would be seen dead in them.

In The Pink

Certain adverts insist real men wear pink but while that may be true, it's not a colour that is traditionally associated with football. Which makes Everton's decision to wear a bright pink shirt complete with a pair of elephants on the chest for their away games in the 2010–11 Premier League all the more mystifying.

Tiger Tragedy

Hull City are also known as the Tigers and it was sadly only a matter of time before some unimaginative designer hit on the ill-advised idea of commemorating the nickname in the form of a new shirt. The new kit was duly unveiled ahead of the 1993–94 season and featured swirling orange and black stripes to mimic a tiger's skin but rather than conjuring images of the majestic big cat, the shirt looked like a hyperactive five-year-old had been unleashed on a paint set.

Keeper Catastrophe

England's pristine white shirt is famous across the football world but anyone unlucky enough to have seen the Three Lions goalkeeper's kit in 1995 and 1996 is probably still trying to erase the atrocious image from their minds. Most infamously worn by David Seaman in the semi-final of Euro 96 against Germany at Wembley, the shirt was a mental montage of purple, green, yellow and red which sadly failed to dazzle the German players enough to make them miss in a dramatic penalty shoot-out.

Jungle Horror

America hasn't always 'got' football and never was that sporting misunderstanding more evident than when a team called the Colorado Caribous took to the field in 1978 in a disgusting white, beige and black kit, complete with hilarious leather tassels around the midriff. The top looked more like a prop from a low-budget western than a football shirt and it obviously didn't do the Colorado players any favours either as the team slumped to 22 defeats and was disbanded at the end of the season.

Comedy Campo

Mexico's first-choice goalkeeper for much of the 1990s, Jorge Campos also fancied himself as something of a fashionista and insisted on designing his own kit for games. The result? A series of horrendous and painfully bright shirts that were guaranteed to induce a blinding headache in any opposition player or fan unwise enough to look in Campos' direction for more than a minute.

Canary Gaffe

Norwich City supporters were forced to take sunglasses with them to home matches in 1993 when their beloved club decided to assault their eyes with an inexcusable yellow shirt with putrid green and white splodges all over it. The kit looked like a flock of incontinent birds had just flown by and proved conclusively that yellow and green are not a good colour combination.

45

SUITS YOU, SIR!

Footballers earn millions these days but all the money in the world can't buy you taste, as the following assortment of badly dressed players conclusively proves.

Skirting Around

David Beckham is widely recognised as one of the world's best-dressed chaps but even he sometimes gets it wrong, particularly when he decided to go for a stroll on holiday wearing a sarong back in 1998. Becks' bold choice didn't catch on and a week later he was back in his Levi's 501s.

Reds In White

Probably the most ill-advised choice of suits ever for the FA Cup Final were worn by Liverpool in 1996 when their bright white Giorgio Armani outfits made them complete laughing stocks. "It was David James' fault we wore white suits," admitted striker Robbie Fowler after the giggling had finally stopped. "He's bigger than everyone so nobody questioned him and at the time he was an Armani model."

Diouf's Disaster

There really is no accounting for taste and Senegalese striker El Hadji Diouf is one of football's serial offenders when it comes to dodgy gear. His worst crime against fashion came in 2010 when he stepped out in an oversized white tracksuit covered in brown spots which made him look like an AWOL Friesian cow.

Frankly, You Look Awful

One of Hollywood's biggest blockbusters of the 1980s was teen romance *Pretty in Pink* but Frank Lampard looking anything but pretty in his choice of bright pink body builder's vest and pink shorts when on holiday in Majorca in 2008. His oversized designer sunglasses were obviously to protect his eyes from the glare of his horrendous outfit.

Dress To Impress

Manchester City's millionaires splashed out on some seriously expensive fancy dress costumes for their 2011 Christmas party and highlights included David Silva in Avatar attire, Gareth Barry as 'Where's Wally' and Joe Hart in full American Football kit. Rumours that Mario Balotelli went as a bag of nuts are probably not true.

Lovely Leia

Plenty of players have gone to the club Christmas party dressed as a character from *Star Wars* but Oxford United's Michael Duberry certainly raised eyebrows when he opted against going as Luke Skywalker or an Imperial Stormtrooper in favour of a Princess Leia costume in 2011. The players who had come as Han Solo quickly made their excuses and went home.

Revolting Rio

It must be something to do with the heat but footballers seem to lose all sense of taste as soon as they disappear off on holiday and Rio Ferdinand was no exception in 2009 when he was spotted in a minuscule pair of blue patterned shorts and a tiny orange top that exposed his midriff and shoulders. The outfit left virtually nothing to the imagination – which is exactly what the England star hadn't used when he got dressed that morning.

Leather Laughter

Chelsea striker Didier Drogba popped over to Munich in 2011 to take part in the nation's legendary Oktoberfest celebrations but obviously had one too many beers after being photographed in a traditional German lederhosen outfit, complete with long white socks and boots. His hangover probably didn't improve when he caught sight of himself in the mirror the next morning.

Punk Kop

Clean-cut Steven Gerrard is rarely seen with a hair out of place but he took a walk on the wild side at Liverpool's 2006 Christmas party, dressing up as a 1970s punk rocker complete with ginger wig, nose rings and tartan trousers.

HAIRY HORRORS

Footballers enjoy a lot of free time. Sadly many of them spend it cultivating some of the most outrageous, gravity-defying and simply ridiculous hairstyles sport has been unfortunate enough to witness, bringing a whole new meaning to the immortal one-liner "on me head, son!"

Wonder Of Waddle

Pop star, mercurial winger, natural entertainer and the owner of arguably football's worst ever mullet, Chris Waddle was a man of many talents – and a terrible, terrible hairstyle. The England star made no apologies for his heinous crime against fashion and as the mullet got longer and longer the sniggers from the terraces grew louder and louder.

Crazy Colombian

Carlos Valderrama's hair was so big he could have stashed a spare pair of shin pads in there and no one would have been the wiser. The legendary Colombian midfielder just loved his blonde, tight corkscrew perm look and as he ran across the pitch, his hair seemed to take on a life all of its own. Suggestions he was actually wearing an elaborate, albeit well-secured wig were met with a stony silence by the man himself.

My Little Pony

Gazza's career was nothing if not colourful and controversial but even by his erratic standards, his decision to get hair extensions and bundle them into a ponytail during his three-year stint in Italy with Lazio was mystifying. Maybe it was the pressure of living in Rome, a city famed for its long-haired men folk. Maybe it was the effect of the Italian sun. Perhaps it was simply a bet. Mercifully the England midfielder quickly realised his terrible mistake and just 24 hours later he jumped on his Lambretta, headed to the hairdressers and demanded the offending extensions were removed.

A Team To Dye For

Individual innovation in the hair stakes is all well and good but the Romanian team raised the bar during the 1998 World Cup when they decided en masse to bleach their hair ahead of their group game with Tunisia. The collective coiffuring was to celebrate qualifying for the knockout stages and the side emerged from the tunnel at the Stade de France in Paris with blonde bonces to a man, presenting the bemused match commentators with one of the toughest 90 minutes of their careers.

Lovely Lalas

Perhaps football's greatest exponent of the flowing mane and goatee combo, Alexi Lalas lit up what was otherwise a tedious 1994 World Cup in the USA with his ground-breaking look. Like Samson, his hair was clearly the source of great strength and the American played a blinder in the tournament as the States reached the last 16. The addition of the hair band merely proved men can accessorise.

Ready And Abel

A man who had almost as many outlandish haircuts during his professional career as the games he played, Portugal international defender Abel Xavier was always eye-catching. Perhaps his most eye-catching creation was this brave bleached-blonde flat top and beard combo.

Green And Mean

Standing at over six feet tall, it was difficult to miss Taribo West but the big Nigerian made absolutely sure he wasn't overlooked by sporting one of the game's most idiosyncratic hairstyles. Shaving most of his head, dyeing his remaining locks green and then gelling them up for an antenna-style look, the defender was undeniably unique.

Killer Kilcline

Brian Kilcline was a beast of a centre-half and he certainly looked the part with his trademark long hair, moustache and goatee that must have been a nightmare to comb. Opposition strikers could have gone missing for days in Kilcline's hirsute offering although rumours that he spent his summers touring with ZZ Top are believed untrue.

TATTOO PARLOUR

Modern players are seemingly addicted to getting inked and these days it's virtually impossible to switch on the television and watch a match without being bombarded with images of footballers sporting endless and increasingly elaborate tattoos.

Happy Families

Mexican winger Nery Castillo obviously loves his parents – so much so that he had his mum and dad's smiling faces tattooed onto his chest. Apparently the ink work shows Mr and Mrs Castillo getting married, so maybe the happy couple at least didn't have to fork out on an expensive wedding photographer.

Mr & Mrs

The 2010 World Cup final will always be remembered for Zinedine Zidane's idiotic head butt on Italy's Marco Materazzi and while the Frenchman would no doubt love to forget the whole thing, the *Azzurri* defender commemorated the match and Italy's victory with a tattoo of the World Cup trophy on his left thigh. His wife Daniela loved it so much that she got a matching tattoo on her right arm but Zidane declined to join the club.

Viking Tribute

Liverpool's Daniel Agger is a qualified tattoo artist so it comes as no surprise that the Danish defender's body is liberally covered in ink. The most impressive part of his body art has to be his back, especially the lower back that depicts the faces of three fierce-looking Viking warriors. Above that are four tombstones, representing the graves of four legendary Danish kings.

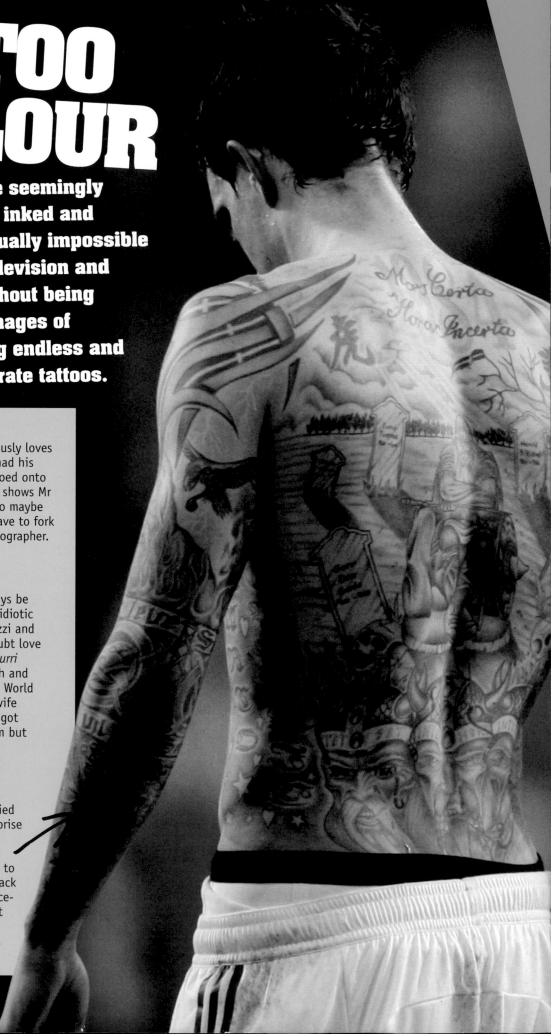

Abbiati Is Loaded

AC Milan goalkeeper Christian Abbiati isn't a man to mess about, judging by the menacing pistol tattoo on his left forearm. He makes sure opposition strikers get a good look at it by insisting on wearing a short-sleeved shirt in matches. Does he think having a gun on his arm would stop rival forwards shooting at him or is it a duel personality thing?

Beckham's Body

Probably the most famous of football's tattooed players, David Beckham first got inked back in 1999 with the name Brooklyn on his lower back following the birth of his first child and since the star midfielder has been adding to his collection on an alarmingly regular basis. His assortment of designs now includes a portrait of Jesus, a ring of roses to celebrate his 10th wedding anniversary and a picture of missus Victoria. If he carries on at the same rapid rate, Becks will soon be getting his big toe tattooed.

Cartoon Capers

Barcelona's Daniel Alves has plenty of standard tattoos dedicated to his family but the Brazilian showed his funny side when he got warring cartoon characters Tweety Bird and Sylvester The Cat inked on the outside of his right ankle.

The Marvel Of Maradona

Say what you like about Diego Maradona but you can't accuse the controversial World Cup winner of lacking in political conviction after he had a portrait of Cuban leader Fidel Castro tattooed on his left leg and a picture of Marxist revolutionary Che Guevara on his upper right arm. Rumours the sly Argentinean was going to get 'I'm A Cheat' tattooed on his right knuckle after his infamous 'Hand of God' in 1986 were probably just wishful thinking.

LONG AND SHORT OF IT

One of the beauties of the beautiful game is that size really is no obstacle to participation and whether you're ridiculously big or surprisingly small, anyone can pull on their pair of boots, emerge from the dressing room and play a match.

Skyscraper Striker

Goalkeeper Kristof Van Hout might be the tallest footballer around but Norwegian striker Tor Hogne Aarøy is the tallest outfield player in the modern game, standing at six feet and eight-and-a-half inches (2.04m). He is a complete menace at corners and dead ball situations.

Belgian Big Guy

The tall kids at school are often told to stand in goal, so it should come as no great surprise that the world's biggest professional footballer – Kristof Van Hout – is also a goalkeeper. Taking up most of the goal, the six-feet-ten-inch (2.08m) Belgian beanpole has earned himself a reputation as a brilliant penalty saver for Willem II, Standard Liege and Kortrijk but is always in danger of banging his head on the crossbar.

Giants Of Brazil

Brazilians have always been big in the football world but the country also boasts the smallest team on the planet. With an average height of just four feet (1.2m), the side in question is made up entirely of dwarves in the north-east region of Brazil which takes on local Under-13 teams in regular friendly matches. Refusing to take themselves too seriously, they're called 'Gigantes do Norte', which translates as the Giants of the North.

Chinese Colossus

It may drive the purists mad but there's no denying that hoofing the ball high and long onto the head of a massive centre-forward can be a highly effective tactic. This makes giant strikers a precious commodity and they don't come any bigger than six-foot-nine-inch (2.06m) forward Yang Changpeng. Nicknamed 'Crouchie' by his friends after the lanky England forward, the enormous front man made quite an impression while on trial with Bolton Wanderers in 2006 but was less popular with the man who had to sit next to him on the flight from China.

The Real Giants

The likes of Real Madrid, Barcelona and Manchester United may be three of the game's biggest teams in terms of trophies, popularity and financial muscle but when it comes to height, the real 'giants' of football are Austrian side SV Mattersburg and Ukrainian outfit FC Volyn Lutsk, regularly towering over their opposition with an average height of six feet one inch (1.85m).

Fantastic Freddy

Striker Peter Crouch holds the record as the tallest player to pull on an England shirt but then you have to go back nearly a century to find the shortest footballer to wear the fabled Three Lions – a certain Frederick Ingram 'Fanny' Walden. A right-winger for Northampton and Tottenham, Walden stood five foot two inches tall (1.57m) and represented England just twice against Scotland in 1914 and Wales eight years later, proving size really doesn't matter.

YOUTH AND EXPERIENCE

There's a saying that if you're good enough, you're old enough and there have been plenty of young footballers past and present who have proved the point. But that doesn't mean the old-timers can't make a difference too...

Leading From The Front

Captains are traditionally one of the more experienced players in a team but American goalkeeper Tony Meola was having none of that ageism nonsense when he took the armband for the USA's World Cup clash with Czechoslovakia at Italia 90 at the tender age of 21 years and 316 days. He still holds the record for the youngest ever skipper in World Cup history while England's Peter Shilton became the oldest captain in the finals when he parked up his wheelchair and led out the Three Lions at the same tournament in the third-place play-off against Italy aged 40 years and 292 days.

Teenage Kicks

Many youngsters spent their time worrying about homework, parties and their parents but Souleymane Mamam had other things on his mind when Togo faced Zambia in a World Cup qualifier in 2001. Mamam was just 13 years and 310 days old when he was selected for Togo for the big match, becoming the youngest ever player to appear in a qualifier. Rumours the Zambia team thought he was actually one of the ball boys are probably untrue.

Boy Wonder

A Bolivian league clash between Aurora and La Paz in 2009 saw history made when 12-year-old Mauricio Baldivieso came on for the final nine minutes of the match, becoming the world's youngest ever professional footballer in the process. Which of course had absolutely nothing whatsoever to do with the fact that the Aurora manager was Baldivieso's dad Julio.

Young Lionel

Midfield maestro Lionel Messi has been rewriting history ever since he broke into the Barcelona first team during the 2004–05 season and one of the first Nou Camp records to fall to the amazing Argentinean was becoming the club's youngest player to score a league goal when he netted in a La Liga clash with Albacete Balompié aged just 17 years, ten months and seven days.

Staying Power

Even if they could you'd expect most professional footballers to hang up their boots long before their 40th birthday but the late, great Stanley Matthews was made of sterner stuff. He was still playing for Stoke City in top flight football at the ripe old age of 50 and his career spanned an incredible 33 years, during which time he made 701 Football League appearances.

55

The Mighty Quinn

Former Oldham, Portsmouth and Newcastle striker Mickey Quinn wasn't at all embarrassed by his ample belly and it certainly didn't stop him scoring more than 200 league goals in his career. Quinn even entitled his own biography *Who Ate All the Pies? The Life and Times of Mick Quinn* but did shed some pounds when he was persuaded to appear in the ITV show *Celebrity Fit Club* in 2006, losing more than four stone to be crowned Mr Fit Club for the series.

WHAT A WAIST!

Professional footballers in the modern era are meant to be models of athleticism and fitness with toned stomach muscles you could bounce a car off but sometimes even the game's greatest players are inevitably tempted by the lure of a burger and chips, stuffed crust pizza and double choc chip ice cream.

Porky Paraguayan

South American striker Salvador Cabañas piled on the pounds during the latter stages of his career but he may well have been comfort eating after the Paraguayan was shot in the head inside a Mexico City bar in early 2010. Luckily Cabañas survived the attack and was able to resume both playing and stuffing his face once again.

Ronaldo Gets Rounder

To be fair to Brazilian star Ronaldo, knee injuries blighted the final years of his playing days but the former Barcelona, Inter Milan and Real Madrid striker obviously spent his long spells on the sidelines gorging himself and as a result quickly if unimaginatively became known as 'Fat Ronaldo' to football fans across the world.

Diego's Diet

After hanging up his boots in 1997, Diego Maradona seriously let himself go and by 2005 he was so obese that doctors advised he undergo gastric bypass surgery. The Argentinean legend duly went under the knife and finally managed to shift some of his excess baggage.

Tubby Tomas

Tomas Brolin was a lean, mean scoring machine in his younger days in his native Sweden but he'd transformed himself into a right porker by the time he signed for Leeds United in 1995 and, carrying far too much extra weight, spectacularly failed to make the grade in the Premier League.

'Big Nev'

Coaches are always telling their keepers to 'fill the goal' and Everton and Wales legend Neville Southall did exactly what he was told, getting bigger and bigger as each of his 17 seasons passed at Goodison Park. 'Big Nev' though was one of the finest goalkeepers of the 1980s and 90s as well as one of the best eaters.

Party Animal

The late, great Ferenc Puskas enjoyed a good party and his indulgent lifestyle meant the Hungarian legend wasn't exactly as svelte as he could have been. When he signed for Real Madrid in 1958, he was 40lb (18kg) overweight but that didn't stop Puskas scoring an incredible 157 league goals in just 182 games for the club.

BENDING THE RULES

The first official laws of football were handed down more than 125 years ago, since when managers and players have been flouting them, while referees sometimes give the impression they've never read them. Football isn't an exact science and, in the heat of battle, mistakes by officials and players are inevitable. It is amazing how often games are notable for controversial decisions, acts of skulduggery or moments of hilarious confusion. Rules, it's said, are made to be broken and in football it seems teams and players will push the boundaries of legality to their limit. But as a famous manager once said, "It's not cheating if you don't get caught!"

Germany's Manuel Neuer is beaten by Frank Lampard at the 2010 World Cup, but the goal isn't given.

CHAPTER 3

The Great Debate

There will perhaps never be a more iconic or controversial goal than the one scored by Sir Geoff Hurst for England against West Germany in extra-time of the 1966 World Cup final and it's a thorny subject that still divides the two countries. Proud Englishmen will never tire of insisting Geoff's deflected shot off the crossbar absolutely, definitely did cross the line while disgruntled Germans are still cursing Azerbaijani linesman Tofik Bakhramov and his terrible eyesight. England fans will celebrate the 50th anniversary of Hurst's heroics in 2016 while German supporters will probably not.

Off The Knee

Most dubious goal-line decisions are controversial but Gonzalo Bazan's disallowed effort for Independiente Rivadavia against Patronato in Argentina in 2011 was just comical. Unleashing a long-range shot, Bazan saw his drive smash against the post but as the Rivadavia keeper turned, the ball rebounded onto his knee and into the goal. Sadly for Bazan, the pinball wasn't over and the ball then hit the stanchion holding up the net and flew out, prompting the bemused referee to wave play on.

GOAL OR NO GOAL?

The debate about goal-line technology has been raging for years and while those who run the beautiful game continue to stubbornly stick their heads in the sand, the number of controversial 'goals' will only continue to grow.

Drawing The Line

No major tournament would be complete without at least one *faux pas* from the match officials, and Euro 2012 was no different. England, not for the first time, were in the eye of the storm when John Terry cleared a shot from Ukraine's Marko Devic in the final group game in Donetsk. Replays proved the ball was over the line but with video technology still absent, the 'goal' was not given and the Three Lions won 1–0. It was something of a novelty for England to be on the right side of a dubious decision, but normal service was resumed when they lost to Italy on penalties in the quarter-finals.

Lucky, Lucky Liverpool

Former Chelsea manager Jose Mourinho dubbed himself 'The Special One' but he certainly wasn't the lucky one when his side faced Liverpool in the semi-finals of the 2005 Champions League. The first leg at Stamford Bridge finished goalless and the return game at Anfield was decided by what became known as the 'ghost goal' after Luis Garcia's close-range tap was given. Countless replays failed to conclusively prove whether or not the ball crossed the line but referee Lubos Michel was convinced, sending Liverpool into the final and Mourinho into meltdown.

Crossbar Karma

Germany were famously on the wrong end of a crucial goal-line ruling in the 1966 World Cup final, but luck was finally on their side in the 2010 World Cup quarter-final against England. Leading 2–1 in Bloemfontein, the Germans thought they'd conceded an equaliser when Frank Lampard's shot hit the crossbar and landed one metre over the line but this time the referee said no and Germany won 4–1.

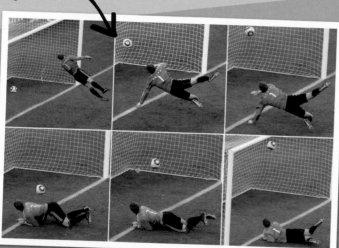

Case For The Corner

Hotly disputed goal-line decisions are frustrating at the best of times but they're absolutely maddening when the ball is not even anywhere near the net. Take for example the game between Watford and Reading in 2008 when a corner resulted in a bit of ping-pong in the Watford box, which was only interrupted when referee Stuart Atwell suddenly whistled for a goal even though the Reading players hadn't appealed. To be fair, the ball had crossed the line – on the outside of the post for what should have been a Reading corner.

Late Arrival

Guilty goalkeepers are always desperate to atone for their mistakes and Tottenham's Heurelho Gomes thought he'd done just that when he let Frank Lampard's soft long shot slip through his fingers and between his legs when Tottenham played Chelsea in 2011, crawling back like a hyperactive toddler as the ball trickled lazily towards the goal. The bungling Brazilian stopped the ball dead on the line but his relief quickly turned to disbelief when the referee wrongly decided he'd got back too late to spare his blushes.

HANDS OFF!

Football is a sport traditionally played with the feet. The clue is in the name. Yet there are always players who find it impossible not to handle the sacred sphere. Some commit the cardinal sin involuntarily, others by pure accident, while there's also a naughty minority who know exactly what they're doing.

Horrid Henry

The legendary luck of the Irish deserted the Republic of Ireland team in 2009 when they were the victims of an inexcusable bit of Gallic cheating from Thierry Henry in their World Cup qualifying play-off game in Paris. With the second leg deadlocked 1–1 on aggregate in extra-time, Henry twice used his hand to keep the ball in play and set up William Gallas for the winning goal. Henry belatedly confessed to his crime but those on the Emerald Isle were in no mood to forgive or forget and demanded a replay. FIFA were deaf to Ireland's pleas because they were busy having lunch, so the French sheepishly headed off to the finals.

Ghana Robbed

Uruguay's Luis Suarez wrote his name into World Cup folklore for all the wrong reasons in South Africa in 2010 when he almost single-handedly sent Ghana out of the tournament. The now infamous quarter-final between the two teams was locked at 1–1 in the dying seconds of extra-time when Ghana's Dominic Adiyah headed what appeared certain to be a dramatic last-gasp winner. Sly Suarez had other ideas and punched the ball away. A red card and penalty duly followed but Asamoah Gyan could not convert for the Africans and Uruguay eventually triumphed in a penalty shoot-out. Suarez was banned for the semi-final but if there was ever a case of the punishment not fitting the crime that was it.

What A Catch

Some handballs are subtle. Some are ridiculously blatant. And then there's the strange case of the clash between Australia and Equatorial Guinea at the 2011 Women's World Cup when Guinea defender Bruna caught the ball in her own penalty area for no apparent reasons after it had crashed against the post. The Australians understandably screamed for a penalty but the bemused referee just stood and watched as Bruna finally realised her *faux pas*, nonchalantly dropping the ball and playing on as if nothing had happened. Despite failing to receive this most clear-cut of penalties justice was done with Australia eventually running out 3–2 winners.

The Hand Of God

The daddy of all handballs, Diego Maradona's infamous piece of skulduggery during the World Cup quarter-final between Argentina and England at Mexico in 1986 remains as big a bone of contention between the two countries as the Falkland Islands. How referee Ali Bin Nasser could believe El Diego (five foot five inches, 1.65m) was able to legitimately outjump Peter Shilton (six foot one, 1.85m, plus his outstretched arms) remains a mystery that would surely defeat Mulder and Scully, while rumours the myopic Tunisian was spotted at the local Specsavers the following day are unfounded. Probably. To be fair, Maradona did score a half-decent second goal with his feet at the Azteca Stadium but England fans don't really like to talk about that one.

Gormless Ghezzal

The 2010 World Cup in South Africa saw one of the most unintentionally comical and idiotic uses of the hand when Tunisia's Abdelkader Ghezzal temporarily lost his marbles and got himself sent off. Ghezzal came off the bench against Slovenia in the 58th minute and within 48 seconds got himself booked for shirt pulling – the quickest yellow card for a substitute in the tournament's history. But worse was to come 15 minutes later when Ghezzal leapt into the air to bring down a high pass, unapologetically thrust his right arm out and handled. The inevitable red card almost flew out of the referee's pocket and within six minutes Slovenia scored the winner against the depleted North Africans. What the Tunisian manager said to Ghezzal in the dressing room afterwards is more than likely X-rated.

Scholes Rumbled

A sly handball in the area can often result in a goal with the referee none the wiser as the 'scorer' wheels away from a mass of bodies to celebrate. It was the complete opposite for Manchester United's Paul Scholes when he smacked the ball into the net with his right hand in a Champions League clash against Zenit St Petersburg in 2008. Scholes wasn't nearly sly enough, rising above everyone and slapping the ball into the net, volleyball-style. The referee wasn't duped and he showed Scholes what was his second yellow card.

ON THE SPOT

The dreaded penalty shoot-out creates instant heroes and villains in equal measure and while it's a favourite with the fans, most players would rather have their teeth pulled out than step up and try their luck.

Goals Galore

By the law of averages it's inevitable a goalkeeper will eventually guess the right way and save a penalty but Argentinean stopper Fernando Gonzalez had the nightmare to end all nightmares in 2009 when he failed to keep out 21 consecutive spot kicks in a shoot-out between Juventud Alianza and General Paz Juniors. To rub salt into the wound, Gonzalez's opposite number Marcos De Tobillas was the first to make a save and then dusted himself off to score the 42nd and winning penalty for a record-breaking 21–20 victory.

Ball Into Space – Part I

All the coaching manuals agree the perfect penalty is hit low and hard. Sadly for England, Chris Waddle obviously never read any of them judging by his sky high effort from the spot against West Germany in the semi-final of the 1990 World Cup, a miss which sent the Germans through to the final and proved the start of the Three Lions' well-publicised misery in major shoot-outs.

Barca Balls Up

Back in 1986 Barcelona were still waiting to win the Champions League for the first time and they blew a golden chance to break their duck against Romanian champions Steaua Bucharest in the final after both sides drew a blank after 120 minutes of tedious, goalless football. Cue a nerve-inducing penalty shoot-out in which the Spanish giants failed to beat keeper Helmut Duckadam once and while Steaua could only manage two successful penalties themselves, it was still enough to lift the European Cup.

Kids Calamity

The Under-10s Derby Community Cup doesn't often hit the headlines but in 1998 it was a competition that sent shockwaves around the world courtesy of the worst penalty shoot-out in history as Mickleover Lightning Blue Sox and Chellaston Boys made a right dog's dinner of proceedings. The Blue Sox eventually won 2–1 but the two teams needed an incredible 66 penalties in the shoot-out before the result was decided, meaning a phenomenal 63 of their efforts from the spot failed to find the back of the net.

Mathematical Mix-Up

Adding up over ten can be tricky if you rely on your fingers and so it proved for one particularly red-faced referee in 2002 when he declared the Dominican All Nations Final over after 11 rather than 12 penalties had been taken. The stunned Zebians team complained that they hadn't actually taken their sixth and last spot kick but the mistaken official stuck to his guns and the Harlem Bombers were crowned champions. Luckily for Zebians, the ref's bosses had spotted his howler and two weeks later the shoot-out was replayed, which they won.

Ball Into Space – Part 2

Roberto Baggio was in sensational form for Italy en route to the final of the 1994 World Cup but his luck well and truly ran out in the shoot-out, blasting his penalty high and wide to spark wild celebrations on the victorious Brazil bench and general sobbing and wailing among his dejected Italian team-mates.

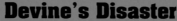

Two-Day Drama

An American High School clash in California between Bishops of La Jolla and San Diego Crawford went on for so long that the match had to be abandoned because of bad light. The two school teams initially kicked off at 3.30pm but with their resulting penalty shoot-out locked at 18–18 at 6pm and with the light fading rapidly, the referee decided they'd have to come back the next day to complete it. Twenty-four hours later battle resumed in the shoot-out once again and after 29 more spot kicks, Bishops finally took the honours.

But I Slipped

Footballers wear studs for a reason and that reason is to stop them slipping at crucial moments – which is exactly what Chelsea captain John Terry did in the 2008 Champions League final against Manchester United. Stepping up to take the fifth and what would have been the winning penalty in a nerve-wracking shoot-out in Moscow, Terry skidded just as he made contact and could barely watch as his effort struck a post and bounced away.

Devine's Disaster

Missing a penalty is embarrassing enough but failing to even get the ball all the way to the goal is every player's nightmare and it's safe to assume Peter Devine has had plenty of sleepless nights after his abject effort for Lancaster City in the 1991 Northern Premier League Division Cup Final shoot-out against Whitley Bay. Striding confidently up to the spot, Devine suddenly got his legs in a terrible, tortuous tangle and his scuffed shot was so weak it only just reached the six-yard box. The crowd of course fell about laughing while Devine tried and failed to save face by feigning injury.

OFFSIDE ODDITIES

The offside law is notoriously difficult to understand. OK, it's not actually rocket science but with the unenviable task of keeping their eyes on the ball, the players and sometimes even on the crowd, even the professionals can make mistakes.

Sheikh On It

'Playing to the whistle' is one of football's most famous clichés but the Kuwait national team took the old saying a little too literally during their 1982 World Cup clash with France when the entire team heard a shrill blast and immediately stopped, assuming the referee had blown for offside. The problem was the referee hadn't actually made a sound and taking full advantage of Kuwait's sudden halt, France scored. Chaos ensued as the Kuwaiti officials stormed the pitch in protest and after he was promised a few hundred barrels of oil, the referee disallowed the goal.

Brolly Bust-Up

Standing all alone out wide, close to the stands isn't always a pleasant experience for linesmen when the locals don't agree with their decisions. Unfortunately things sometimes get ugly and assistant referee Aguilar Rodriguez found this out to his cost when he was hit by a flying umbrella from the terraces during a 2011 Spanish Primera Liga clash between Granada and Majorca, cutting his face. Luckily referee Clos Gomez took pity on his blood-soaked colleague and ordered everyone off the pitch, abandoning the game.

Soviet Sickener

Diego Maradona's 'Hand of God' made the headlines during the 1986 World Cup but the tournament was not without more controversy and those who witnessed the USSR's last-16 clash with Belgium are probably still scratching their heads after the clueless linesman failed to spot Jan Cuelemans was at least five yards offside when he scored a crucial late equaliser for the Belgians. The outrageous 'goal' took the match into extra-time but justice was definitely not done as the Belgians clinched a 4–3 victory.

Banter Backfires

British television commentators Richard Keys and Andy Gray fell foul of the offside law in 2011 after being caught off-air taking the mickey out of lineswoman Sian Massey. "What do women know about the offside rule?" said Gray. "Somebody better get down there and explain offside to her," replied Keys. After their exchange was made public, the pair apologised but it was too late to save their bacon and they were sacked. Massey probably didn't send them a 'Good Luck' card either.

Flag Day

Technically referees don't actually have to take any notice of their linesmen but official Ray Tinkler should certainly have been less stubborn when he took charge of Leeds United's crucial clash with West Brom in 1971. Late on Baggies striker Colin Suggett surged forward but the Elland Road crowd breathed a huge sigh of relief when the flag rightly went up for offside only for terrible Tinkler to overrule his linesman and waive play on. West Brom of course scored and despite Don Revie's desperate attempts to get the linesman to have a word with Tinkler, the goal stood and Leeds crashed to a defeat that cost them the title.

Hakem's Header

Referees are there to make sure the players abide by the rules of the game. They are definitely not there to break them themselves but no one had told Turkish official Atan Hakem when he took charge of the 1986 Superlig clash between Besiktas and Ankaragucu, scoring the winner for Ankaragucu in the final minute of the game with an accidental header. To make matters even worse, Haken was standing in a blatant offside position when he nodded home but rather than do the decent thing and chalk his bizarre effort off, he awarded the goal and trotted sheepishly back to the centre circle.

Hands Up

If you're going to appeal for offside, it's a good idea to do it all at the same time, as Newcastle United did in their Premier League clash with Manchester United in November 2011. Their synchronised show of hands worked a treat, 'persuading' the linesman to chalk off Javier Hernandez's 'goal'.

Strip Shocker

Plenty of players remove their shirts to celebrate a goal but Austrian coach Adi Pinter decided to get his kit off before kick-off in 2011 when his FC Pasching side faced his former club Grazer AK. In a bizarre and misguided show of loyalty to Grazer, the bonkers 63-year-old boss removed his shirt to reveal the letters GAK written on his back but his antics failed to inspire his players and Pasching were thrashed 6–0. The club weren't impressed either and Pinter was sacked after the match.

Head Banger

Head injuries are an occupational hazard for footballers but Yugoslavia's Rajko Mitic managed to bang his bonce before the start of his nation's 1950 World Cup clash with Brazil, colliding painfully with an overhanging metal girder as he raced out of the tunnel at the Maracana Stadium. With blood pouring from his wound and feeling understandably dazed, Mitic sat out the first half of the game and as it was an era when substitutes weren't allowed, Yugoslavia had to play with 10 men for the first 45 minutes. Mitic managed to stagger on for the second half but was powerless to stop Brazil strolling to a 2–0 victory.

Diana's Debacle

Celebrities love to get involved in major football events but legendary singer Diana Ross probably wishes she hadn't after providing one of those hide-behind-the-pillow moments at the 1994 World Cup opening ceremony. All the Motown legend had to do was mime her way through a song before kicking a ball into an open net from three yards out, breaking the goal in two on impact and releasing a thousand white balloons in the process. Sadly Ross scuffed her shot wide of the target in spectacularly bad style but despite probably the worse miss in World Cup history, the show carried on regardless.

KICK-OFF TIME

Fans don't always have to wait until the referee blows his whistle and the first ball has been kicked for the matchday entertainment to begin and all sorts of oddities and accidents can occur when the crowd – and the players – are least expecting them.

Money Matters

The toss up before kick-off rarely produces any great drama but referee Gwyn Owen managed to raise eyebrows ahead of the 1982 clash between England and Northern Ireland at Wembley when he nearly did himself a mischief with his own coin. Owen had to take evasive action to avoid the flying cash, proving that money really is the root of all evil.

Kicking Up A Stink

Manchester United had a stinker at Sunderland in 2010 when a sewage pipe above their dressing room burst just before kick-off. Part of the ceiling collapsed and smelly water rained down on the team, delaying the start of the match by 20 minutes. "I think my suit is in the skip," said United defender John O'Shea after the sudden and unwelcome downpour. "It will have to be burned for health reasons."

Cry Baby

Playing at the World Cup Finals can be an emotional experience but crying your eyes out in front of billions of watching fans around the globe is still embarrassing. North Korea striker Jong Tae-Se shot to worldwide fame in 2010 when TV cameras captured him blubbering his way through the entire national anthem before their clash with Brazil. The fact that he put his dry-eyed team-mates to shame with some, well, unashamed patriotism, was all the more surprising given the fact that he was actually born in Japan to South Korean parents.

It All Kicked Off!

A 2011 Singapore League clash between Hougang United and Etoile FC had to be abandoned before a ball had been kicked in anger when players from both sides scrapped with one another in what proved to be football's most bad-tempered warm-up. One of Etoile's balls strayed into the Hougang half of the pitch but as keeper Antonin Trilles went to collect it, a row broke out and within seconds head butts, punches and kicks were being exchanged by players and staff from both clubs and the referee decided he just couldn't face 90 minutes more.

One Team In Tallinn

There's something missing from this picture; it's Estonia, who didn't turn up for their home World Cup qualifier against Scotland in Tallinn in 1996. An argument about floodlighting meant the match was moved to the afternoon but Estonia refused to play. As their fans sang, "There's only one team in Tallinn," Scotland kicked off and 'scored', but the referee called off the game.

STRICTLY NO DIVING

Considering football is played almost exclusively with your feet, it's remarkable how hard some players find it to stay on them. The slightest touch can send them crashing to the ground in 'agony', but we don't have to believe they're actually hurt.

Blow Me Down

Despite being a big, strong fella, Didier Drogba has a reputation as being, ahem, a 'little unstable on his feet' and for every goal the Ivory Coast striker has scored in his career, there have been incidents when he's suddenly hit the turf and the crowd have turned in unison to see exactly where the sniper was hiding this time.

Meier's Madness

Managers are meant to set a good example to their players but Duisburg boss Norbert Meier did the complete opposite in 2005 when his side faced Bundesliga rivals Cologne, stopping opposition midfielder Albert Streit from taking a quick throw-in. The pair squared up and after the faintest of touches of the forehead, both men flung themselves backwards as if they'd been karate kicked by Jackie Chan.

Double Trouble

If at first you don't succeed, try and try again is a saying that Equatorial Guinea's Narcisse Ekanga Amia certainly took to heart during the 2012 African Cup of Nations, twice feigning injury to get the referee's attention. The midfielder's first dive (and scream) was rudely ignored by the official so Amia The Actor sat up to check whether anyone was watching and then promptly threw himself back down on the grass, rolling around like a dying penguin. A stretcher was despatched to rescue the poor little soldier but after just moments on the sidelines, he made a miraculous recovery and returned to the fray.

The Anti-Dive

Footballers aren't all bad though and back in 1997 Robbie Fowler showed admirable honesty after he stumbled over Arsenal goalkeeper David Seaman and was awarded a controversial penalty. The Liverpool striker immediately got to his feet and gesticulated to referee Gerald Ashby that he should not award his side a spot kick. Despite this, the official forced Liverpool to take the penalty and although Fowler's kick was saved, Jason McAteer banged in the rebound. It was win-win for Fowler though when he was later handed a Fair Play Award by UEFA.

An Official Dive

Play-acting is clearly a bug that's catching in Brazil and even the referees aren't immune from it. During a Fourth Division clash between Operario and Mirassol in 2011, referee Rodrigo Nunes de Sa brandished a straight red card to a Mirassol man, who reacted by moving his head towards the man in black. After gently making contact, the official threw himself backwards and hit the deck like he had just been hit by a sniper. Players from both sides didn't like what they saw and riot police were summoned to keep the angry mob at bay.

Belgian Bungle

It's not always easy to tell when someone is faking it on a football pitch but when a player is lying unconscious on the turf, the likelihood is they might actually be genuinely hurt. This pearl of wisdom however clearly passed a Belgian referee by as he brandished a red card at Hainaut star Julien Lecomte for 'simulation' in a lower league clash against USG Quevy in 2012 much to the bemusement of everyone inside the stadium after it emerged that a stray elbow in the neck had displaced three of Lecomte's vertebrae.

X-RATED

There has always been a dark side to football and no matter how many red cards are dished out, certain players will always cross the line in their desperate quest for victory. Which means the beautiful game can sometimes become very ugly indeed.

Bare Bones

One of the most sickening sights ever seen on a pitch, Norbert Siegmann's studs-up challenge on Ewald Lienen during a brutal 1981 Bundesliga clash between Werder Bremen and Arminia Bielefeld was so vicious that it sliced open the player's leg and exposed the bone. Lienen was not amused when the physio offered him a plaster for his injury.

Keane's Kick

Revenge is a dish that is meant to be best served cold and patient Manchester United hardman Roy Keane waited for a full three-and-a-half years before he took retribution against Leeds' Alf Inge Haaland after the pair had clashed in a previous game. Keane finally got his revenge in 2001 in the form of a blood-curdling challenge that bent the Norwegian's knee backwards and ended his career. The Irishman later admitted in his autobiography that he'd deliberately set out to 'hurt' Haaland and he was given a £150,000 fine.

Elbow Gloom

Swinging an elbow can seriously damage a footballer's health and former Portsmouth midfielder Pedro Mendes found this out to his cost when he was knocked out cold by Manchester City enforcer Ben Thatcher in 2006. Mendes collapsed into the advertising hoardings after Thatcher unleashed a flying elbow and the medics had to use oxygen to revive him. The Portuguese then suffered a seizure in the ambulance on his way to hospital but at least Thatcher was handed an eight-match ban for his awful and unlawful assault.

Balls Up

It's never nice being hacked to the ground but that really doesn't give a player the right to slam his studs straight into the perpetrator's crotch. Athletic Bilbao's star midfielder Pablo Orbaiz did just that however to Getafe's David Cortes in 2010, delivering a sharp stab to his 'gentleman's area' which left the shocked Spanish defender bent over in obvious agony.

Gazza's Gaffe

Adrenaline is great if you can harness it, but it is a handicap if you can't. Paul Gascoigne definitely couldn't control himself in Spurs' 1991 FA Cup final clash against Nottingham Forest, launching into a kamikaze tackle on Gary Charles. This was Gazza's second bad foul of the match, but it did more damage to himself, forcing the Tottenham star off after just 17 minutes. Gazza tore his cruciate ligaments with his reckless challenge and he spent the next 12 months in the treatment room rather than on the pitch.

Stamp It Out

Some players just can't resist having a second 'pop' at an opponent and that was definitely the case in 2002 when Leeds United's Lee Bowyer swept Malaga defender Gerardo's legs from beneath him in a Champions League encounter at Elland Road. Gerardo hit the grass but bad boy Bowyer decided he hadn't done enough damage and decided it would also be a good idea to tread on his adversary's head too. It wasn't and although he was only shown a yellow card at the time, UEFA reviewed the video evidence and slapped him with a richly deserved six-game European ban.

Battiston Battered

Violence on the pitch is usually punished with a sending off or a ban but German goalkeeper Harald Schumacher got off scot free after his reckless jump into French forward Patrick Battiston during the 1982 World Cup semi-final. Schumacher's horrendous challenge left Battiston in a coma with two missing teeth and a broken neck. The referee saw no foul and simply restarted the game with a goal kick.

MEN IN BLACK

The life of the football referee is rarely an easy one and sooner or later they will make mistakes. Unfortunately for the game's outnumbered and oppressed officials, what happens next is totally out of their control.

Sozzled Shmolik

The pressures of refereeing are enough to make any stressed official indulge in a post-match drink but Belarusian whistler Sergei Shmolik turned to the bottle before kick-off in 2008 with disastrous results. Refereeing a league clash between Vitebsk and Naftan, Shmolik was so tipsy that he spent most of the match staggering around the centre circle, refusing to issue a single card despite some tasty tackles, and when post-match tests revealed he was seriously over the limit the Belarusian FA promptly suspended him.

Card Crazy

The 2006 World Cup tie between Portugal and Holland promised to be interesting, but Valentin Ivanov made it crazy. In a game of only 25 fouls, the Russian referee showed Mark van Bommel a yellow card after two minutes and Khalid Boulahrouz one five minutes later. By the final whistle, the yellow card count was at 16, with two players from each side being sent off after receiving two cautions. Maniche kept his shirt on after scoring the only goal – just as well seeing he'd already been one of those booked.

Junjie Rumbled

Referees are meant to be unfailingly neutral but China's Huang Junjie let the side down. In 2009 he took a bribe to fix a match between Shanghai Shenhua and Sydney FC, then said he had fixed a 2007 clash between Shenzhen FC and Manchester United. The Chinese FA rumbled him and Junjie was fined £200,000 and banned for life.

Perfect Pierluigi

The most famous referee of his generation, Pierluigi Collina was as distinctive looking as he was strict. The Italian official reached the peak of his profession when he took charge of the 2002 World Cup final between Brazil and Germany. Collina now trains the next generation of Italian whistlers, as well as appearing in TV adverts. As long as they're not for hair products.

Out For The Count

Incidents of referees accidentally getting in the way of the ball are common but Khalid Ramsis must have wished he'd been more alert during a Moroccan league fixture between DHJ El Jadida and struggling FUS Rabat in 2009, ending his afternoon's work in hospital rather than his dressing room. Poor old Ramsis fatally failed to see Fussiste Souiyat's fierce 35-yard half volley coming and was hit so hard that he suffered serious head and neck injuries and missed the rest of the season.

Dangerous Dane

Awarding a penalty is often controversial and as German referee Herbert Fandel learned in 2007, it can also prove potentially painful. Fandel was officiating a Euro 2008 qualifier between Denmark and Sweden in Copenhagen when he gave the visitors a late spot kick, prompting outraged Danish fan Ronni Norvig to invade the pitch and try and punch him. Luckily for the referee, a Danish player stepped in to save him. The game was abandoned, Sweden were awarded a 3–0 win and Norvig was fined £210,000.

African Assault

Upsetting players is an occupational hazard for referees. Getting beaten up by an angry mob though is certainly not what officials sign up for but sadly this is just what happened to unlucky Israel Munjuni in 2012 when he took charge of the match between Young Africans and Azam FC in Tanzania. Munjuni had already sent off one Young African player and when a second saw red, the rest of the team lost the plot and attacked him, forcing the game to be stopped for several minutes as security guards jumped in to defend the outnumbered official.

Yellow Peril

Everyone knows that two yellow cards equals an early bath. Everyone that is except English referee Graham Poll who disastrously decided to rip up the rulebook during the 2006 World Cup in Germany when he showed Croatia's Josip Simunic three yellows before finally giving him his marching orders against Australia. Only Poll knows why he didn't send Simunic off after his second yellow but the penny did finally drop when the Croatian committed yet another foul and the forgetful Englishman scribbled his name down in the book yet again.

CHAPTER 4

THE BIG MATCH EXPERIENCE

The action out on the pitch is only part of the big match experience for supporters and even if the game on offer isn't exactly a thriller, fans can frequently get their all-important entertainment fix from some unlikely and hilarious sources. Extreme and sometimes dangerous weather conditions, crazy stadiums, bizarre animal invaders and even hot-headed mascots can all enliven a dull and dreary match just when the crowd is losing the will to live and thinking about leaving early. So the next time you're bored at a game, keep your eyes peeled and whether it's a sudden bolt of lightning, an over-enthusiastic police dog or a wolf versus pigs punch-up, you never know what might happen next.

Republic of Ireland fans do the 'Poznan' dance in that city during their Euro 2012 match against Italy.

WEATHER WARNING

Football is traditionally an outdoor sport, which means the beautiful game frequently finds itself at the mercy of Mother Nature and her array of extreme climatic conditions. Little wonder then that so many matches over the years have had to bow down to the power of the natural world.

Light Show
England's eagerly anticipated 1990 World Cup clash with the Republic of Ireland didn't really need any added entertainment but Mother Nature couldn't resist contributing at the Stadio Sant'Elia in Cagliari. This dramatic bolt of lightning kept the crowd on their toes.

Wind Of Change
Footballers occasionally have to duck and dive to avoid various objects thrown at them by idiots in the crowd but the officials and players of the Black Leopards and Orlando Pirates in South Africa were faced by a far greater (and sizeable) threat in 2007 when strong winds starting blowing the hoardings at Ellis Park, Johannesburg, onto the pitch. It gave a whole new meaning to the power of advertising.

Muddy Hell
It's not just the conditions on match day that can cause havoc for the players, as this shot of Ian Wright and Paul Gascoigne proves as they trained at Izmir in 1993 ahead of England's World Cup 94 qualifying clash with Turkey. To be fair, the fact Gazza voluntarily dived into the mud and then pushed Wright in didn't exactly help keep their kits clean.

Indian Chilli

Some players take prudent precautions against extreme weather but the Indian footballers who went to the 1952 Olympic Games in Finland were just asking for trouble when they insisted on playing the tournament in bare feet. Unsurprisingly the sub-zero conditions inside the Pallokenttä Stadium in Helsinki quickly took their toll and India were thrashed 10–1 by Yugoslavia in their opening group game. Worse still, several players suffered frostbite to their exposed toes and the Indian FA wisely decided that in future, boots would be a jolly good idea for their team.

What A Scorcher

Indian summers are for most an unexpected bonus but for Manchester City's players back in September 1906, an unseasonable heat wave was a real nuisance when they faced Arsenal in a League game. The clash was played in sweltering temperatures of more than 90°F and five City players couldn't cope, crawling off the pitch suffering from heat exhaustion. Arsenal kept their cool and won 4–1.

Is There Anybody Out There?

A healthy crowd of 63,499 squeezed into St James' Park for the FA Cup clash between Newcastle United, the holders, and Swansea Town back in 1953 but the two sets of fans only saw eight minutes of action before the game was abandoned. The culprit was a thick, impenetrable layer of fog that came out of nowhere. When the referee realised he had absolutely no idea how many players were actually on the pitch, he blew his whistle and groped his way back to the changing rooms.

White Out

The players of AZ Alkmaar and Ajax Amsterdam had to dig out their thermals and gloves in 2008 when the snow descended on their Dutch league clash, which no doubt explains why both teams appear to be kicking a giant orange around the pitch. Of course – goalkeepers apart – they were the lucky ones, as they kept warm chasing the ball for 90 minutes. Pity the poor, unprotected fans who sat in the bitter cold.

Woodwork Catastrophe

These days clubs are well equipped in terms of spare balls, corner flags and even fourth officials but back in 1895 things were altogether more basic and the clash between Darwen and Leicester had to be abandoned after just two minutes when a vicious wind suddenly blew across the pitch. The gust dislodged a crossbar and with no spare to hand to replace the wrecked woodwork, the game was prematurely called off.

Stone Me

You'd be forgiven for associating Africa with withering heat but it was an altogether different climatic phenomenon that made headlines in Uganda in 2010 when the Mbale Heroes and Gulu United FC crossed swords. The league game was an hour old when giant hailstones suddenly began to rain down on the players and the crowd and with visibility reduced to a few feet and heads getting sore, the officials decided to call it a day and look for some much-needed shelter.

Lights, Camera, Inaction!

Instances of floodlight failure are far from rare in football but the sudden loss of illumination is usually the result of a blown fuse or someone's failure to pay the electricity bill. The abrupt darkness that fell upon Hibernians' pre-season friendly with Raith Rovers in 2009 however was the result of a freak electrical storm which knocked out the lights just 40 seconds into the second half, forcing an early end to proceedings.

Raindrops Keep Falling On My Head

Unlike silly summer sports like cricket and tennis, football games tend to continue whatever the weather throws at them. Someone should really have told that to Blackburn goalkeeper Brad Friedel as he desperately clasped his hands together over his head. Sadly they were never going to keep him dry as the rain poured down on him.

Shake, Rattle & Roll

Manchester United's pre-season tour of the Far East in 2005 took an unexpected and frightening turn in Japan when they played the Kashima Antlers side in Tokyo – an earthquake rocked the National Stadium. The surprise tremor hit midway through the second half and once the United players worked out it wasn't Sir Alex Ferguson shouting at them from the touchline, they realised it had to be an earthquake. The Antlers won the game 2–1 and the United players reluctantly headed to the dressing room to face a furious Ferguson and another, albeit man-made, seismic event.

Replay Relapse

It's not unusual for matches to be postponed during the winter months but the 1979 Scottish Cup game between Inverness Thistle and Falkirk had to be rearranged an incredible 29 times because of persistent snow and ice. The original date for the game was early January but the clubs had to wait 47 days until the Kings Mills ground was eventually declared playable in late February, by which time both sets of players were already planning a much-needed summer holiday.

Storm Stops Play

They say a little bit of rain never hurt anyone but when it's accompanied by terrifying bolts of lightning and enormous and ominous claps of thunder, it's definitely wise not to take any chances. This is what the UEFA bosses decided when an apocalyptic storm engulfed Donestsk moments after the start of Ukraine's match with France at Euro 2102. The players took refuge in the dressing rooms while the supporters huddled together at the back of the stands for shelter. The match resumed after a 55-minute delay, much to the relief of TV pundits worldwide. After only four minutes of play they had almost run out of things to discuss.

Swimming Lessons

Countless games have had to contend with the odd rain shower but Sao Paulo's match with Palmeiras in 2011 witnessed such a torrential downpour that the fans were literally swimming in the water-filled concrete stands of the Morumbi Stadium before kick-off. Rivers of water cascading down through the terraces quickly filled the bottom rows of seats but amazingly the match still went ahead after a 70-minute delay – only for another interruption in the second half when the water got into the electrics and caused a floodlight failure.

81

NO PLACE LIKE HOME

Every team needs somewhere to play and whether a club is big or small, there really is no place like a home stadium. But not all grounds are the same and as the following examples prove, even football stadiums can have unusual and sometimes unbelievable claims to fame...

In The Clouds

If you ever make the long trek to watch Peruvian side Union Minas, it would be a good idea to take an oxygen tank with you as their ground – the Estadio Daniel Alcides Carrión – is the highest in professional football. The ground is an incredible 14,300ft (4,380m) above sea level and the air up there is so thin that visiting teams have complained that Union enjoy an unfair advantage.

Colour Co-ordinated

Football's answer to the chameleon, the Allianz Arena in Bavaria hosts games for both Bayern Munich and TS 1860 Munchen and the ground's designers came up with a cunning plan to make both teams feel at home with an innovative lighting system on the outside of the stadium. So when Bayern play, the ground is lit up in red but it all changes to blue when TS 1860 have a game and it can even transform to white when the German national team are in town.

Artistic Arsenal

When Arsenal decided to knock down the North Bank of their old Highbury Stadium back in the early 1990s, the club didn't want the two teams on the pitch faced with an ugly building site during the rebuilding work and hit on the cunning idea of constructing a giant mural of Gunners supporters to cover up the hard hats and builders' bums. Sadly, the first mural did not reflect the club's multi-racial fan base, so it had to be completely repainted with a politically correct representation of the supporters.

Green Agenda

The grass is usually the greenest thing inside a football ground but the Estádio Janguito Malucelli in Brazil is the exception to the rule and not a single drop of concrete or an ounce of metal was used in its construction, earning the unusual venue the nickname the 'Brazil Eco-Stadium'. The main stand was built on a hill with the seating cut out of the earth and only recycled wood was used for the changing rooms and other buildings.

Hollywood Honour

Austrian side Sturm Graz were so proud of the silver screen success of local boy Arnold Schwarzenegger back in 2000 that they decided to name their home ground in honour of the home-grown muscleman. Sadly however the Arnold Schwarzenegger Stadium ceased to be five years later when the town and its favourite son fell out after the Governor of California refused to stop an execution over in the USA and the club decided to drop his name and rebranded the ground as the UPC-Arena.

Rock And A Hard Place

It cost £70 million to build the Estádio Municipal de Braga in Portugal for the 2004 European Championships, which is hardly surprising when you realise the constructors had to shift millions of tonnes of rock to build the stadium. With a capacity of just over 30,000, the ground is nestled in an old quarry and behind one of the goals, there is an eye-catching wall of natural stone.

Chocolate Cash

[text largely illegible]

Automobile Anarchy

Plenty of stadiums 'moonlight' as venues for other sports and once a year the Schalke Arena in Germany forgets all about football and transforms itself into a Total Stock Car Racing track. Nearly 50,000 cram into the arena to watch the cars roar around while the groundsman stares on in a mixture of disbelief and horror.

Closest Neighbours

There are many cities across the world that boast two or more teams but however fierce the respective rivalries, nowhere can compete with Dundee in Scotland in terms of the closeness of the stadiums. Dundee play at Dens Park while Dundee United play at Tannadice and as the crow flies there is a mere 100 yards between the nearest corners of the two grounds, ensuring that the 'away' fans never get lost en route to a Dundee derby.

Ancient View

A solid defence is a vital ingredient for any successful side and Croatian side HNK Trogir certainly knew all about repelling unwelcome invaders at their Igralište Batarija Stadium, boasting a 15th-century castle complete with ramparts at one end of the ground. Trogir folded in 2009 but before going out of business, fans could book a table at the castle's restaurant and watch the game, although throwing hot oil at opposition teams was strongly discouraged.

What A Site

Wearing a hard hat is mandatory on building sites for health and safety reasons, but no one taken the time to warn West Ham and Newcastle players as they walked onto the pitch at Upton Park in 2001. Luckily the rubble was only on the sidelines as the Hammers' home underwent a facelift. No players fell victim to the type of untimely workplace accident that required the dubious services of ambulance-chasing lawyers.

Sunny Disposition

Power cuts have ruined countless matches but it's not a problem for teams playing at the Kaohsiung National Stadium in Taiwan thanks to the ground's 8,844 solar roof panels that generate enough electricity to keep the ground's 3,300 lights and two giant television screens burning into the night. Used for the Women's Olympic Qualifying Tournament in 2011, the stadium has a capacity of 55,000 and as long as the clouds do not descend, never has to pay an electricity bill.

Sliding Sensation

A good slide tackle can be a thing of rare beauty but it's the entire pitch at the Sapporo Dome in Japan rather than the players which does the sliding. Built for the 2002 World Cup final, the stadium boasts a retractable 8,300 tonne pitch which can be slid in and out of the home to ensure the turf is not on hand when the weather is poor. It can also make the 42,000-capacity ground versatile enough to convert from football to baseball and back again.

On The Water

Some would argue that the game's modern superstars think they can walk on water and if they played a game at The Float at Marina Bay in Singapore, they literally could. A floating platform measuring 390 feet by 270 feet and weighing in at 1,000 tonnes, the float can hold up to 9,000 people in a grandstand. For football matches, a 2022 World Cup draw between England and Wales FC demonstrated the unique experience of playing on the world's largest floating stage.

ANIMAL ANTICS

The beautiful game and the animal kingdom do not usually mix and judging by these bizarre, frequently painful and sometimes fatal incidents, it's a policy both football and our furry and feathered friends should stick with.

The Loose Goose

They might not look particularly threatening but an angry goose can certainly pack a punch when it's in a bad mood as Rochdale goalkeeper Neil Edwards found out in a match against Scunthorpe in 2004. Stunned by the sudden arrival of an uninvited Canada goose on the Glanford Park pitch, Edwards tried to remove it but the old bird was not for turning and he got a nasty nip on his arm for his troubles that needed medical attention. The crowd cried fowl but Edwards wasn't laughing.

Bovine Bother

Most animals that invade the pitch get there by accident but the two cows who grazed the grass at the Amsterdam Arena in Holland in 2001 were released on purpose. By the club's own fans. After the Arena turf was replaced 24 times in just five years, the supporters were so fed up with the playing surface that they sent out the cows in protest.

Canine Capers

Dogs are supposed to be man's best friend but a police Alsatian on duty in Germany in 1959 was far from friendly when Fortuna Dusseldorf striker Dieter Woske slid into the goal trying to convert a cross. He bit down on the unfortunate player's shorts but, luckily for Woske, it was the dog and not him who had his collar felt. The over-enthusiastic dog was dragged away and the match continued.

Fox In The Box

Old Firm games between Celtic and Rangers are never dull but a 1996 clash was even more entertaining than usual when a fox suddenly ran onto the pitch. Both sets of players tried to grab the intruder but the fox was far too quick for them.

Marauding Moggy

If cats really do have nine lives, the frisky feline that brought a halt to proceedings during Liverpool's Premier League showdown with Tottenham in 2012 probably used up at least one of his after scampering onto the Anfield pitch in front of 40,000 fans before he was eventually captured by a steward. Later renamed Shankly, the stray cat was such a hit with spectators that within hours of his unscheduled 15 minutes of fame, his spoof Twitter account had more than 30,000 followers.

Run, Rabbit! Run!

The Spanish word for rabbit is 'conejo' and that's what the players of Real Madrid and Real Betis all shouted in 1997 when one of the big eared fellas was thrown from the stands at the Bernabeu. The two sets of players gave chase but it was Madrid's Carlos Secretario who caught the roaming rabbit. "Secretario may or may be not a good player," joked the match commentator, "but he is indeed a great hunter."

He Must Be Nuts

Squirrels are famed for burying nuts, which could explain why one of their number suddenly appeared on the pitch during Arsenal's Champions League semi-final clash with Villarreal at Highbury in 2006. The bushy-tailed rodent was obviously looking for a stash of pecans and just couldn't wait for the final whistle.

Shower Time

Most players love a refreshing shower at the end of a match but England legend Jimmy Greaves unfortunately 'enjoyed' an unscheduled and far less pleasant downpour after apprehending a stray dog during the 1962 World Cup quarter-final against Brazil. With no one seemingly able to intercept the canine interloper, Greaves got down on all fours to work a bit of animal psychology on the mutt before grabbing it by the collar. The dog however had the last laugh as he 'went to the toilet' all over the England striker.

Fowl Play

Blackburn fans weren't exactly overjoyed when their club was bought by the Venky's – an Indian poultry company – and decided to demonstrate their disapproval at Ewood Park in 2012 by releasing a chicken onto the pitch. Blackburn, however, were still relegated while the fate of the poor chicken remains unclear.

R.I.P. Mistar

Some unexpected animal invasions are pure comedy but others are just tragic and the sad case of Indonesian footballer Mistar was certainly the latter when he was killed at the age of 25 after a herd of wild pigs overran his team's rural training pitch in 1995 with fatal consequences.

Moose On The Loose

Animals don't always have to venture onto the pitch to make an impact, as Norway defender Svein Grondalen discovered while out jogging during the 1970s. A famed fitness fanatic, Grondalen's run was interrupted when he came across a sleeping moose, who was none too pleased to be woken up and charged. Grondalen took evasive action but gashed his leg as he fled and was out of action for weeks.

Stung Into Action

Bored goalkeepers are usually grateful for any distraction to liven a dull 90 minutes but Bayern Munich and Germany stopper Oliver Kahn probably could have done without the wasp sting that had him writhing in agony in a cup clash with Werder Bremen in 2007. Officials first thought Kahn had been hit by a missile thrown from the stands but the penny dropped when the angry Bayern star asked for a can of insecticide and a rolled-up newspaper.

Brodie's Body Blow

Dogs are meant to be man's best friend but there were certainly no thoughts of friendship on Chic Brodie's mind back in 1970 after the Brentford goalkeeper collided with a stray sheepdog during a game against Colchester, shattering a knee cap and bringing his playing career to an abrupt and premature end. "The dog might have been a small one," Brodie said years after the accident, "but it just happened to be a solid one."

Lucky Ducky

Getting hit by a football can often sadly spell the end for one of our feathered friends. However the duck struck by a ball during the Finnish first division clash between TPS and KuPS in 2011 had a friendly fireman to thank for its miraculous recovery. The bird was knocked unconscious by a corner taken by KuPS midfielder Seth Ablade and it looked doomed until a local fire fighter stepped in to try to save it. For a few minutes it was was touch and go for the duck, but it was revived and flew off.

Rude Cow

The reserve team clash between Potterspury and Southcott in Buckinghamshire in 2011 was not what anyone would call a high-profile event but there was one very special 'guest' in the shape of a two-tonne cow, which decided she wanted to play. Emerging from a gap in the hedge in one corner, the escapee from a nearby farm began charging the players before 'relieving' herself in the middle of the pitch and it was only after the two teams had shooed her away and then found a bucket and spade for an emergency clean-up job that the big game could continue.

MASCOT MAYHEM

Dressing up as a cartoon character or oversized animal and dancing wildly on the touchline is the bread and butter of those tortured souls who spend their weekends working as football mascots. No wonder then that sometimes they go just a little bit crazy...

Mind The Post

What's better than one mascot at a match? A whole bunch of mascots running around the edge of the pitch at half-time, raising money for charity of course. Such was the scene at the 2010 Colchester versus Southend game but it was an evening to forget for hapless Larry the Lion, who forgot to look where he was going and crashed head first into one of the goalposts.

Silly Swan

At 10 foot tall, it was impossible to miss Swansea mascot Cyril the Swan but he certainly made himself even more conspicuous in 1998 during an FA Cup game with Millwall, sprinting onto the pitch to celebrate a goal with a dance before throwing his wings around scorer Martin Thomas. The home crowd loved it but the Football Association of Wales were not amused and slapped big Cyril with a £1,000 fine and a touchline ban for his antics.

Fairytale Fracas

In the famous fairytale, the Wolf and the Three Little Pigs were not exactly the best of friends and it was the same old story in 1998 when Wolverhampton Wanderers travelled down to face Bristol City at Ashton Gate. The Wolves mascot Wolfie tried to 'borrow' a ball from City's Three Little Pigs, who took exception and much to the horror of the wide-eyed children in the ground who thought Wolfie's aggression was limited to a bit of blowing, a fight broke out. The four were promptly ejected although Wolfie was obviously unrepentant and strode out to the theme tune from *Rocky* at Wanderers' next home game.

Cup Ambush

It's one of the oldest tricks in the book. Someone kneels down behind 'the victim' while someone else pushes them from the front, sending them tumbling helplessly to the turf. It's been done countless times and it made it onto live TV in 2012 when broadcaster ESPN were covering the FA Cup clash between Sheffield Wednesday and Blackpool and the Wednesday mascots Barney and Ozzy Owl cruelly sneaked up on the ESPN FA Cup mascot and did the dirty deed.

Beauty And The Beast

Mascots are an integral part of the half-time entertainment at a game but Aston Villa's Hercules the Lion failed to strike the right note during his team's game with Crystal Palace in 1998, allowing his paws to 'roam' rather too freely as he cuddled Miss Aston Villa and getting himself the sack. "I growled and then grabbed Miss Villa around the waist with my paws and pulled her around a bit," explained Hercules, AKA Gavin Lucas. "It was a bit of a grapple and a bit of a hug. Then I gave her a kiss but it wasn't much of a kiss because I still had my lion's head on."

Playing With Fire

Manchester City's striker Mario Balotelli is famous for his madcap stunts and mischievous sense of humour, so it was no great surprise when the impudent Italian just couldn't resist grabbing the tail of a dinosaur mascot at the 2011 Dublin Super Cup in Ireland and giving it a pull. The dragon, it must be said, wasn't very impressed but there certainly is no truth in the rumour that Mario's radical hairstyle was the result of a singe of his fringe by the angry mascot.

MEET THE GAFFER

If the players are football royalty, then the manager is the King. After all, he's the man who picks the team, decides what formation to play and then shouts incessantly from the touchline for 90 or 120 minutes, seemingly on the verge of a heart attack. This is a celebration of the frequently mad men who mastermind what we watch every week, the larger-than-life personalities who take flak from fans and the media when things go wrong and who are usually only a defeat or two away from losing their jobs. From their bizarre training techniques and questionable dress sense to mind games and occasional dugout meltdowns, managers are the game's great characters and without them, football is little more than 22 men or women running around like headless chickens.

Barcelona boss Pep Guardiola is flying high after his side beat Manchester United in the 2011 Champions League final.

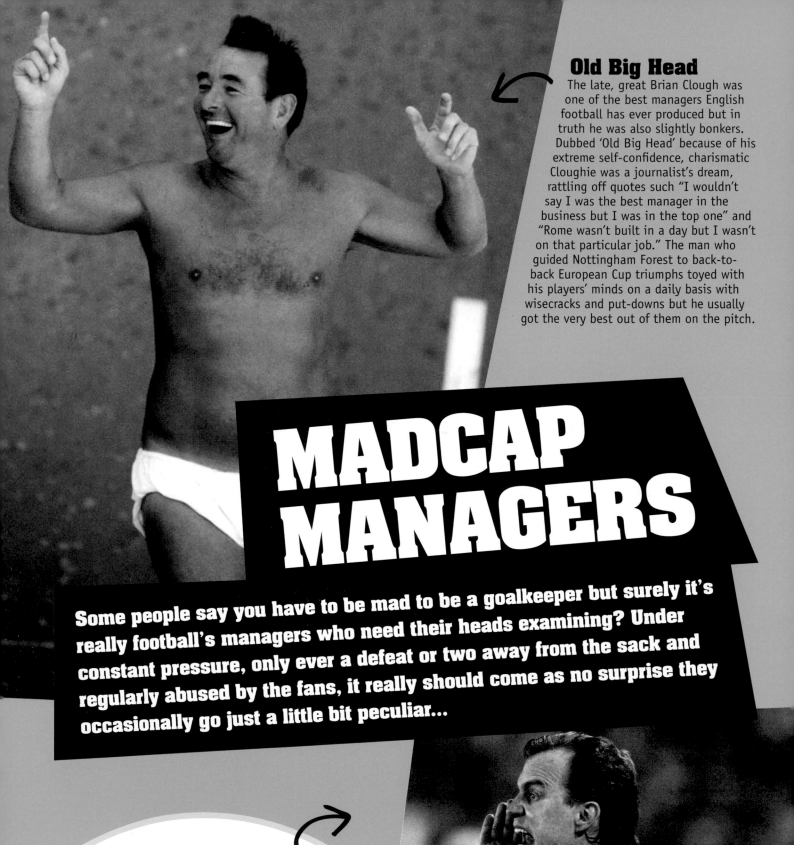

CHAPTER 5

Old Big Head

The late, great Brian Clough was one of the best managers English football has ever produced but in truth he was also slightly bonkers. Dubbed 'Old Big Head' because of his extreme self-confidence, charismatic Cloughie was a journalist's dream, rattling off quotes such "I wouldn't say I was the best manager in the business but I was in the top one" and "Rome wasn't built in a day but I wasn't on that particular job." The man who guided Nottingham Forest to back-to-back European Cup triumphs toyed with his players' minds on a daily basis with wisecracks and put-downs but he usually got the very best out of them on the pitch.

MADCAP MANAGERS

Some people say you have to be mad to be a goalkeeper but surely it's really football's managers who need their heads examining? Under constant pressure, only ever a defeat or two away from the sack and regularly abused by the fans, it really should come as no surprise they occasionally go just a little bit peculiar...

Going Loco

Nicknamed 'El Loco' (or the 'Crazy One'), Argentinean coach Marcelo Bielsa proved over the years there is genuine method to his obvious madness and among his crazy ideas he likes to make his defenders and strikers train at different places at different times and is also happy to conduct four-hour press conferences. Bielsa was also the Argentina manager for the 2002 World Cup and as preparation for the tournament ordered his players to watch 700 football DVDs before booking them into the worst hotel he could find.

Please Leave A Message

Known for his swearing and straight-talking, no-nonsense style, former Wimbledon boss Joe Kinnear surprised many in the English game when it emerged that he had recorded this message on his answer phone in 2008. "I'm out at the moment but should you be the chairman of Barcelona, AC Milan or Real Madrid, I'll get straight back to you. The rest can wait." Whether any of the three chairmen in question did ever call remains a mystery

Nighty Night

Pioneering manager Helenio Herrera was one of the first to use psychology in a bid to motivate his players, pinning slogans and cryptic messages around the training ground and stadium when in charge of Atletico Madrid, Inter Milan and Barcelona in the 1950s and 1960s. Off the pitch he was also a rather strict disciplinarian and sent club staff to players' homes to check that they were asleep at the time he had demanded.

Tactics? No Thanks!

Bulgarian legend Hristo Stoichkov was an awesome player in his heyday at the 1994 World Cup but his management style was not quite as well received at club or national level. As coach of the national Bulgarian side between 2004 and 2007, he forced three players into early retirement, accused Romania of fixing a match and left fans scratching their heads at the bizarre 2-4-4 formation he decided to deploy in an international against Malta. Miraculously he was still appointed manager of Spanish side Celta Vigo in 2007 and when he was unveiled to the local media, Stoichkov announced "I don't believe in tactics." He was sacked six weeks later.

It's In The Stars

Most sane managers regard current form and fitness as two of the most important criteria for their team selection but former France manager Raymond Domenech saw things a little differently. The astrology devotee believed heavily in the power of the stars and as a result, he didn't like to pick players with the Scorpio or Leo star signs. "When I have got a Leo in defence I've always got my gun ready as I know he's going to want to show off at one moment or another and cost us," said the troubled Frenchman.

Hilarious Holloway

King of the one-liners, Ian Holloway is an undisputed master of conjuring the comedy phrases and earned himself cult hero status as Blackpool manager in the process, leading the side to victory over Cardiff in the 2010 Championship Play-Off Final and declaring after the final whistle, "I couldn't be more chuffed if I were a badger at the start of mating season."

Messing About On The River

The conventional approach to football management never appealed to English boss Martin 'Mad Dog' Allen. With a penchant for swimming, Allen swam across the River Trent before his Notts County side faced Nottingham Forest in 2011 and while in charge of Brentford, he fined his players £1 each for failing to follow him in a dip across a stream before they took on Hartlepool United. And when he wasn't popping on his trunks and getting wet, Allen once had his players practising set pieces in a motorway service station en route to a league fixture.

Air Play

First impressions always count and Swedish legend Pia Sundhage certainly created quite a stir when she took over as manager of the USA Women's team in 2007. Addressing her squad for the first time, Sundhage suddenly brought out her air guitar and began singing Bob Dylan's "The Times They Are A-Changin'" but not content keeping her questionable musical skills between herself and the four walls, the ever-smiling Swede even started playing her imaginary guitar on the touchline during the 2011 World Cup in Germany.

Give Me The Mic

Unconfined joy can do funny things to people and in the case of Phil Brown, it suddenly and embarrassingly made him think that he was a brilliant singer. Ecstatically celebrating Hull City's survival in the Premier League in 2009, Brown ran onto the pitch at the KC Stadium, grabbed the nearest microphone he could find and began belting out a verse of the Beach Boys classic "Sloop John B", screaming "I don't wanna go home, this is the best trip I've ever been on." The stunned crowd, who'd just watched their team lose narrowly to Manchester United, understandably didn't know whether to laugh or cry.

The Special One

The most charismatic manager of the modern era has to be Jose Mourinho. Suave, confident and rather successful, the Portuguese coach is good, and he knows it. After shooting to fame in 2004 after racing down the side of the Old Trafford pitch like an over-excited puppy en route to a famous Champions League triumph over Manchester United with FC Porto, Mourinho joined Chelsea and immediately told the watching world: "Please don't call me arrogant but I'm European champion and I think I'm a special one." Controversy has loyally followed Mourinho ever since but unsurprisingly, the outspoken coach refuses to change his style for anyone.

Wally With The Brolly

To be fair to Steve McClaren, the former England manager wasn't exactly renowned for his madcap antics but he will forever be remembered as the 'Wally with the Brolly' after sheltering from the rain at Wembley as his side crashed to a disastrous 3–2 defeat to Croatia in 2007. The result saw England fail to qualify for Euro 2008, got McClaren the sack after just 18 games and ensured no future England boss would dream of carrying an umbrella ever again. He later was ridiculed when, as coach of Dutch club FC Twente, he addressed a press conference before a Champions League match against Arsenal in heavily Dutch-accented English.

Chop It Off!

Former Argentina boss Daniel Passarella had his own views on how footballers should look and he wasn't for turning. Earrings were immediately banned by the hardliner when took up the reins in 1994 and next in the firing line were the players with long hair. After several run-ins with hirsute stars like Gabriel Batistuta, the manager took it even further by refusing to select in-form Fernando Redondo for the 1998 World Cup squad after the midfielder refused to cut off his own lovely locks.

Airline Antics

It's great to see managers refusing to take themselves too seriously and John Spencer, the boss of MLS side Portland Timbers, definitely didn't do that in 2011 when he agreed to appear in a TV advert. Spencer posed as a short-tempered steward for a local airline company, taking a day off from shouting at his players to shout instead at the passengers.

'Big Mal'

One of the most flamboyant characters ever to manage in English football was the late Malcolm Allison, best known for his two spells in charge of Manchester City in the 1970s. The man dubbed 'Big Mal' once hired a steeplejack to climb onto the roof of Old Trafford, home to City's rivals Manchester United, to lower their flag to half-mast for a joke. He was also seen drunkenly ice skating on Wimbledon Common, encouraged his players to drink champagne instead of beer and forced his players to occasionally train in gas masks to increase their lung capacity. When it comes to big personalities, few were bigger than Allison.

It's My Ball!

Manchester City manager Roberto Mancini is usually a placid character but the supercool Italian completely lost the plot during a Premier League clash with Everton in 2010, rugby tackling opposite number David Moyes in his technical area after the Scot refused to give the ball back. Mancini decided to wrestle Moyes for the missing ball but their little game of hide-and-seek was brought to an abrupt end when referee Peter Walton told them to both grow up and sent them to the stands.

DUGOUT CAPERS

Old-fashioned wooden benches may now have given way to luxury leather arm chairs and plastic roofs but the dugout is still the manager's domain and it remains a hotbed of raw emotion, comic capers and furious fights that just aren't for the faint-hearted...

Blagging It

Ticketless Republic of Ireland fan Conor Cunningham was so desperate to watch his side's crucial clash with Estonia in Tallinn in 2011 that he decided he'd try a bit of theft and then impersonation to watch the match. First the 27-year-old stole an Estonian team tracksuit and after walking past security guards posing as one of the substitutes, he then calmly sat next to Estonian manager Tarmo Ruutli. Cunningham recorded the game on his mobile phone but was eventually rumbled by stewards after trying to order a pint of Guinness.

Sausage Subs

Football clubs are always looking at new ways to make money but few have been as forward thinking as Spanish club Sevilla, who decided to accept sack loads of Euros from a local meat company in 2012 in return for remodelling their dugout as a giant hot dog. The roof became the sausage, complete with twirls of ketchup and mustard, while the back of the bench was transformed into the bun. It looked bizarre but certainly made the crowd unusually hungry.

Sleepy Head

It's understandable when substitutes lose interest in a game, especially when they've got no chance of actually kicking a ball in anger, but falling asleep is just asking for trouble. Just ask Real Madrid's Julien Faubert, who was so bored by his side's 3–2 victory over Villarreal that he decided to grab 40 winks during the game. Perhaps he was dreaming of making a rare appearance for the team?

Computer Capers

Italian forward Mario Balotelli is regarded as one of the biggest 'characters' in football but even he excelled himself in 2011 when he decided it would be perfectly acceptable to mess about with his iPad while sitting on the bench during Italy's Euro 2012 qualifier against the Faroe Islands. Whether he was playing *FIFA 12* or *Angry Birds* is unknown but after getting rumbled by the TV cameras, Italy team official Gigi Riva actually defended the silly striker. "He only played a few minutes against the Faroes, so he couldn't do much," Riva said, presumably with a straight face.

Manners Cost Nothing

Allowing television cameras to film a manager 'in action' in the dugout is a risky business, as former England boss Graham Taylor found to his cost in 1993. Taylor was disastrously filmed questioning one of the referee's decisions in a crucial game against Holland at Wembley and the microphones caught him telling the linesman "I was just saying to your colleague, the referee has got me the sack. Thank him ever so much for that, won't you?" The most polite protest in the history of the game perhaps but Taylor's prediction came true and later that same year he lost his job as England failed to qualify for the 1994 World Cup finals.

Water, Water, Everywhere!

Football's all about kicking a ball and if angry Arsène Wenger had stuck to this simple premise in 2009, the Arsenal manager wouldn't have found himself in the stands. The Frenchman was so angry after his side had a goal disallowed against Manchester United at Old Trafford that he took his frustration out on an innocent water bottle in his technical area, launching it several feet into the air. Referee Mike Dean however was not impressed and sent him to the stands, resulting in Wenger comically clambering over the top of the visitors' dugout to watch the last few seconds of the match.

In God's Name

Managers have always known it's best to avoid swearing at match officials but in 2010 Verona coach Domenico Di Carlo became the first Serie A gaffer to be punished for taking God's name in vain after the Italian FA decided it wasn't going to stand for anyone showing any religious disrespect. Caught on camera in his technical area screaming a 'blasphemous expression', the Verona boss was handed a one-match touchline ban and ordered to say five Hail Marys.

Head Banger

The 2011 Mexican Cup semi-final between Morelia and Cruz Azul descended into violence when an irate Cruz Azul fan ran onto the pitch to pick a fight with one of his own players and while the outnumbered referee struggled to control a series of bad-tempered brawls, Azul keeper Jesus Corona made his way towards the opposition dugout for a 'chat' with Morelia assistant manager Sergio Martin. At first it seemed as if the pair were holding hands enjoying a friendly conversation but TV cameras then caught Corona kick Martin in the groin before landing a head butt into his face.

Mind The Gap

Jose Mourinho is usually a rather cool dude but the Real Madrid manager was left distinctly red-faced during a match at Getafe in 2011 when he was tripped up and unceremoniously floored by the steps inside the visitors' dugout. The Getafe supporters roared with delight while Mourinho demanded a mirror to check his hair and suit were still in place.

Republic Rage

In those dark times before football's ever-so-helpful 'fourth officials' rode out of the sunset to save the day, managers used to hand slips of paper with the substitutions they wanted to make straight to the linesmen. In a 1994 World Cup finals match between the Republic of Ireland and Mexico, a FIFA official decided to grab the slip from Ireland boss Jack Charlton and, deliberately or not, delayed the introduction of striker John Aldridge. The move sparked a 'frank' exchange of words from all concerned in the technical area before Aldridge finally got onto the pitch to score a late consolation goal.

Sit-Down Protest

When Bayern Munich were running rings around Manchester City in their Champions League group stage clash in Germany in 2011, Argentinean striker Carlos Tevez ignored the pleas of his manager to come on and play after deciding he'd prefer to have a nice sit-down in the dugout rather than get a bit sweaty and his shorts dirty. City fined Tevez six weeks' wages, pointing out the job of a footballer was, well, to play football.

You're Fired

Who needs an oak-panelled boardroom for making the big decisions when you've got a decent dugout going spare? That was clearly the thinking of the men in charge at Spanish side Villarreal in 2012 after watching their side's loss to Levante, descending to the dugout after the game to discuss the future of under-fire manager Jose Molina. The omens for Molina were not good and after a quick chat on the bench, the president and vice-president decided to give him the boot.

IT WORKED IN TRAINING!

Most football folk believe a training session is all about fitness and finesse but other more forward-thinking managers and players have come up with far more innovative ways of getting ready for the big game...

Say Your Prayers!

Plenty of players have prayed for divine intervention during a match but the pupils of St Joseph's Convent School in Bradford back in the 1960s got some holy help *before* the kick-off. They were coached by Sister Gabriel, a nun with a penchant for the beautiful game. However, there is no record of the team ever needing the 'Hand of God' to win their matches.

Let There Be Light

Accuracy in front of goal is the Holy Grail for strikers desperate for glory and lucrative contracts and German marksman Miroslav Klose definitely hit on a novel way of improving his shooting ahead of the 2006 World Cup finals. Klose shunned the training pitch and headed home, working on his close control by turning lights on and off by kicking a ball at the switches. Mrs Klose was not amused but her hubby's 'light bulb' moment worked a treat and he finished the World Cup as top scorer with five goals.

The Tutu Technique

Ballet and football are not natural bedfellows but the two did reluctantly join forces in 2004 when Queens Park Rangers headed off to the English National Ballet to get some unlikely tips on flexibility and stamina from the dancers. Disappointingly the embarrassed QPR players refused to don the tutus on offer but after a few pirouettes, they headed back to Loftus Road to insist on long-distance runs only in future.

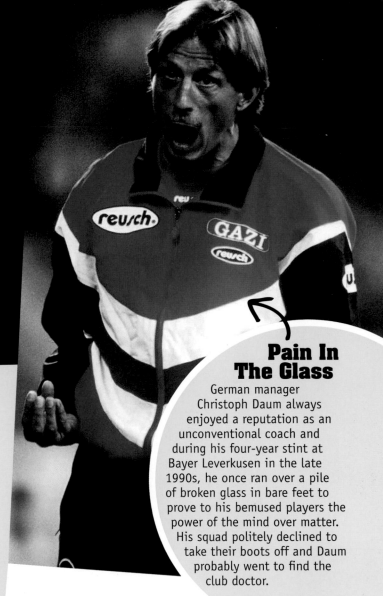

Naked Ambition

Every footballer is desperate to get noticed and Romanian striker Adrian Patulea certainly raised a few eyebrows in 2008 when he turned up uninvited at Lincoln City's training ground. But it wasn't his silky skills that caught manager Peter Jackson's attention. "He was spotted by the groundsman running around the training ground with his girlfriend on his back," Jackson explained. "The trouble is his girlfriend was naked which got the attention of the players." Patulea's trick worked and he got himself a contract.

Cold Comfort

Footballers don't like the cold, which means the Motherwell players during the reign of Mark McGhee must have been utterly miserable after their boss ordered them to take off an item of clothing each time they missed a shot in training. McGhee wanted his squad to get used to the extremes of the Scottish weather while the players started arriving for training wearing eight vests each.

Pain In The Glass

German manager Christoph Daum always enjoyed a reputation as an unconventional coach and during his four-year stint at Bayer Leverkusen in the late 1990s, he once ran over a pile of broken glass in bare feet to prove to his bemused players the power of the mind over matter. His squad politely declined to take their boots off and Daum probably went to find the club doctor.

Bridge Of Sighs

The Humber Bridge is one of the longest in the UK and when Phil Brown was the manager of Hull City in the 2000s, it was also where you could see the Tigers squad doing a series of shuttle runs in training. Brown hoped the spectacular setting would inspire his team while the players speculated whether they could survive jumping off the bridge to escape.

Fright Night

The 'fear factor' is a phrase frequently used in football. It is one that Barnet manager Martin Allen took very literally as he prepared his side for an FA Cup first-round clash at home to fellow non-league club Stalybridge Celtic in November 2003. He took his players off to the cinema to watch horror classic *The Texas Chain Saw Massacre* on the night before the big game. After the spooked squad were removed from behind their seats, 'having a nightmare' was appropriate as Barnet were held to a 2–2 draw, but they went through to the next round by winning the replay 2–0.

Egg Chasers

The reign of Co Adriaanse as manager of Dutch side AZ Alkmaar in the early 1990s was nothing if not eventful. During one session he ordered his players into their cars, drove them 13km from the training ground and then confiscated their keys and ordered them to run back. But 'Psycho Co', as he was affectionately known, really lost the plot when he inexplicably told his players they were having an Easter egg hunt in training. After an hour, no eggs had been unearthed and Adriaanse informed his, ahem, 'egghausted' players that he hadn't actually hidden any.

TOUCHLINE CATWALK

All eyes are usually on the 22 men running around in shorts chasing the ball but certain managers don't like to feel left out and whether they mean it or not, what they are wearing frequently becomes more interesting than the match itself...

Boot-Iful Boss

Norwegian manager Egil Olsen made quite an impression when he became Wimbledon boss in 1999, not least because of his penchant for wearing wellington boots. The eccentric Scandinavian hated driving and could be seen walking to training in scruffy wellies and he often chose to don the unusual footwear on the touchline during matches too. The boots were such a hit that the club shop even began flogging Olsen Wellies before he was sacked less than a year later.

The Disasters Of Dunga

Former Brazil coach Dunga was a persistent offender when it came to crimes of touchline fashion. The Samba legend would mix and match dated leather jackets with all sorts of weird and wonderful baggy shirts but perhaps his biggest *faux pas* came in 2007 during a friendly against Portugal. His attire was so bad that he was quizzed by journalists afterwards and Dunga revealed that his extremely dodgy grey patterned shirt (complete with fake braces) had been created by his daughter, a trainee fashion designer, and he was taking family loyalty to extremes.

Scarf Mania

Trendsetting Italian Roberto Mancini looked so good in his 1950s-style Manchester City scarf that it sparked a meltdown during Christmas 2009 with the club's shop simply unable to keep up with the demand from fans desperate to re-create the same, suave look. The City boss even had the club's hierarchy copying him by sporting the same style in the Etihad directors' box.

Ahead By A Neck

It's not just high-profile managers that have an eye for fashion, as Exeter City's Paul Tisdale has proved after becoming a cult hero in Devon thanks to his consistently sophisticated attire. Famed for his trademark cravat, the Grecians boss is also known to sport a sheepskin flying hat on occasion too and back in 2007, thousands of Exeter City fans wore Tisdale face (and cravat) masks for the Conference Play-Off Final in honour of their dapper boss.

Looking Mean In Green

The late Brian Clough was voted 'worst dressed manager in English football history' in a 2005 newspaper poll for his persistence with what appeared to be the same old green jumper, worn over the course of many years as boss of Nottingham Forest. It may not have been particularly fashionable but Cloughie's attire is one of the most iconic in the game.

Jogi Blue

German fans were simply obsessed by their national team coach Joachim Loew during the 2010 World Cup Finals but it was his fashion sense and not tactics that got the nation talking. Sporting a rather fetching v-neck sweater on the sidelines for each game, Loew sent thousands of women into a mad frenzy and even 'created' a new shade of colour in the process. Sales of 'Jogi Blue' jumpers went through the roof to such an extent that Germans were even popping over to bordering Holland to pick up the summer's must-have garment.

Sleeping Bag?

Every winter the usually dapper Arsenal manager Arsene Wenger lets himself down by choosing a three-quarter-length puffa jacket that's big enough to keep half of the Gunners squad warm. Oversized and with no shape to it whatsoever, it has quite rightfully been compared to a sleeping bag. Aren't the French supposed to fashionable?

Expensive Overcoat

As Chelsea's manager, Jose Mourinho's 'lucky' grey overcoat earned him admirers from all around the world, so much so that it was auctioned for £22,000 in 2005 and now hangs proudly in the museum at Stamford Bridge. Since leaving the Blues the fashion-conscious icon has ditched the trademark suit and tie he used to wear underneath his coat, opting instead for a smart casual jumper with trousers look.

FANTASTIC FANS

Supporters are what football is all about. If they didn't turn up in their millions, players would feel unloved, turnstiles would be dismantled and clubs' accountants would be sobbing over their calculators. Of course, not all fans are always on their best behaviour and whether it's those who suddenly decide to show the world everything they've got when they streak or the supporters who just can't resist a cheeky pitch invasion, fans sometimes get just a little bit too close to the action. But let's face it, most supporters are happy to have their fun in the stands and whether it's with flamboyant fancy dress, daring dancing or funny flags, they always make sure they make their mark on match day.

South Africa supporters get to work on their vuvuzelas during the 2010 World Cup finals.

CHAPTER 6

FOOTBALL CRAZY

For some people football is a religion. For others it's much more serious than that and wherever you are in the world, you can guarantee you'll find fanatical fans who simply cannot live without their regular fix of the beautiful game.

Travel Costs

Following your team home and away can be expensive and England super fan Brian Wright has had to dig deep. He had spent £100,000 to see 248 England games over 22 years, then found another £10,000 to get to South Africa for the 2010 World Cup. "Some people will think I'm crazy," he said. "But watching England is not just about 90 minutes of football, it's about being part of something."

Bridal Dash

Your wedding day is meant to be one of the most important days in your life but Mrs Olivia Gosney had football rather than confetti and cakes on her mind in 2012, racing straight from her nuptials to Fratton Park just in time for a Championship clash between her beloved Portsmouth and Derby County, who rather marred the day by winning 2–1.

Match Maniac

Englishman Brian Buck went to his first football match when he was just four and became so hooked on the beautiful game that he spent the next 55 years going to as many games as possible. Incredibly he racked up his 10,000th match in 2011, which works out at a staggering 694 whole days of his life spent on the terraces. "I'll do this until my dying day," he said after setting his marvellous milestone. "I hope I can make it to 15,000 at least. I still hope to make 20,000 but that's some task."

Crazy Colombian

Sunglasses were a must for Colombia's game with Bolivia during the 2011 Copa America in Argentina, judging by this colourful Colombian fan who certainly claimed the award for most cumbersome costume. The sponsorship probably covered the cost of his ticket but spare a thought for the unfortunate supporters who had paid to sit behind him for the whole match.

Outrageous Orange

Eating carrots is supposed to improve your eyesight, especially at night time, so this vegetable-toting Dutch supporter probably didn't miss any of the action when the Netherlands took on the Czech Republic in the group stages of Euro 2004 in Portugal. Sadly what he actually saw was a 3–2 defeat for his team. Fanatical Dutch supporters liven up any atmosphere, especially those dressed from top to toe in their national colours, though seeing a six-foot carrot approaching you can be a bit unnerving.

Sticky Situation

Collecting football stickers is a rite of passage for many fans. In 2011 these Birmingham supporters amassed so many they covered a car in them, then embarked on a six-day, 2,000-mile drive – for charity – around Europe. It took more than 5,000 stickers to redecorate the 12-year-old Ford Escort Finesse, which probably doubled the value of the £200 motor in an instant.

Kung-fu Keeper

Eager stewards and fleet-footed policemen are the natural enemies of the adventurous pitch invader but the Dutch Cup clash between Ajax and AZ Alkmaar in 2011 proved that irate goalkeepers can be equally dangerous. The keeper in question was Alkmaar's Esteban Alvarado, who took violent exception to a foray onto the pitch by a 19-year-old Ajax fan, flooring him spectacularly with a kung-fu kick. Alvarado put the boot in twice more as the teenager lay prone – just seconds before the referee showed him the red card.

Wheels In Motion

Last-gasp goals can make even the most level-headed supporter go a bit crazy, which is exactly what happened when Northampton Town equalised against Rotherham United at the Sixfields Stadium in 2011. Cue teenager Derry Felton, who drove his motorised wheelchair across the pitch in celebration and in the process became an instant internet hit. "I didn't know what was happening and then I was in the middle of the pitch and I just thought, how did I get here?" Felton admitted. "It was just a spur of the moment thing and I never thought it would end up on YouTube."

KEEP OFF THE GRASS

The pitch is supposed to be the exclusive preserve of 22 players, the match officials, hyperactive managers in their technical areas and exuberant mascots desperate for their 15 minutes of minor fame. However, the hallowed turf is sometimes also forced to accommodate uninvited intruders and impostors...

"They Think It's All Over..."

The most iconic of all pitch invasions, the England supporters' impromptu dash onto the Wembley pitch during extra-time of the 1966 World Cup final, was probably a result of nervous energy and we should be thankful that none of them blocked off Sir Geoff's legendary left-foot thunderbolt strike at the death. Whether they really thought it was all over (as the BBC's Kenneth Wolstenholme famously put it) remains a mystery but the fact the two teams were still out there, kicking the ball, should surely have given them a clue.

Cousin Capers

Football talent can often run in the family so when an 'agent' rang Southampton boss Graeme Souness in 1996 claiming to represent Ali Dia, a cousin of African superstar George Weah, the Saints manager quickly handed him a one-month deal. Dia made his debut against Leeds as a 32nd-minute substitute but was so spectacularly bad, he was taken off 21 minutes later. It later emerged Dia was no relation whatsoever to Weah and Souness retreated to the dressing room to rip up the contract.

Women Only

Some pitch invasions can have unintended consequences and that was certainly the case when the notoriously boisterous fans of Turkish side Fenerbahce trampled the turf en masse in one of their side's 2011 pre-season friendlies. The Turkish Football Federation was not amused and decided to ban the club's male supporters for two games for their indiscretion. The result? A record crowd of 43,000 women and children turning out for Fenerbahce's league clash with Manisaspor in Istanbul a few months later. "The women were a lot more passionate and a lot more encouraging," conceded club vice-president Ali Koc after the game.

Power Prank

The pre-match team photo is an old tradition and back in 2001 it presented Mancunian prankster Karl Power with the ideal opportunity to pull off one of the most audacious pranks in football history when Manchester United faced Bayern Munich in the Champions League. Power got past security by pretending to be part of a TV crew and once pitch side at Old Trafford, he changed into his kit and casually strolled out with the rest of the United players for a photo. He was only rumbled when a quick-witted young fan couldn't find Power in his Panini sticker collection.

Wembley Whammed

The history of Scottish invasions of England can be traced back over many hundreds of years but one of the most famous came in 1977, when the Three Lions hosted the boys in blue at Wembley in the final game of the Home International Championship. Thankfully there weren't any claymores in plain sight – or at least used – but the Tartan Army fans still more than made their presence felt after their team had triumphed 2–1 to be crowned champions that year, streaming onto the field at the final whistle to begin the celebrations. Some of the supporters thought the crossbar would make a perfect souvenir of the day and pocketed pieces of the woodwork while others, obviously aware that the Wembley pitch was due to be relaid after the match, generously decided to save the overworked ground staff the bother and began ripping up the turf so that it could be 'relocated' north of the border. Many a Caledonian garden or window box was partly re-layed with a little piece of Scottish football history.

Folklore fans

It probably didn't take fans too long to hit on the idea of dressing up as leprechauns during the Republic of Ireland's Euro 2012 campaign but what their fancy dress may have lacked in originality, they more than made up for with effort. Whether the leprechauns of Irish folklore actually wore sunglasses is a mystery.

Rock & Roll Rodgers

Mischievous British bookmakers insisted there was more chance of Elvis Presley being spotted alive than Swansea City avoiding relegation from the Premier League in the 2011–12 season but the Welsh side proved them wrong, surviving the drop comfortably. And just to remind the bookies of the error of their ways, Swans boss Brendan Rodgers called on the club's fans to come to the last home game of the season dressed as 'The King', leading to an acute shortage of Elvis costumes in the Principality.

Mankini Ban

When England played Kazakhstan in a World Cup qualifier in 2008, Wembley authorities banned fans from wearing the mankini made famous in the movie *Borat*.

DRESSED FOR THE OCCASION

Showing sartorial support for your team is usually limited to wearing a replica shirt or donning a club scarf. However, for some of the more flamboyant football fans, the more outrageous the matchday outfit the better.

Dubious Doppelgangers

Many supporters yearn to be just like their favourite player and two Bayern Munich fans at the 2012 Champions League final against Chelsea thought it would be a laugh to come as the club's star player, Franck Ribery. The wannabe lookalikes replicated the French winger's trademark goatee and crooked teeth perfectly, but they certainly went far beyond the lines of decency by emulating the facial scars Ribery had suffered in a childhood car crash.

Scandinavian Cross-dresser

This vocal Viking could be seen in the colourful crowd cheering Sweden on during their Euro 2012 clash with Ukraine in Kiev. He/she proved once and for all that there simply isn't a fancy dress outfit that's too outrageous for a match. The costume also had an added and surprising benefit at half-time when the fan didn't like the look of the queue for the men's toilets.

Cartoon Capers

When Hartlepool United headed to London to play Charlton Athletic in a League One encounter in 2012, the Valley faithful were stunned to see 171 Smurfs pour into the stadium just before kick-off. The band of Belgian cartoon characters were of course United's travelling support, who opted to all dress up as Smurfs in tribute to their team's blue and white strip although the two conspicuous fans at the front who opted to buck the trend and come as Robin and Bananaman obviously didn't get the right message before setting off from the north-east.

Why The Y-fronts?

While some fans prefer to dress up for the big match, supporters of Japanese Division One side Kashiwa Reysol decided to strip down to their underpants for their local derby with Kashiwa Antlers in 2000. Exactly why they disrobed has been lost in translation but they certainly made an impression, despite the man in the middle wearing sunglasses and a scarf letting the side down.

FLARES AND FLAGS

Pundits love to refer to how great goals can 'light up' a game but some supporters prefer to literally illuminate proceedings, ignoring the fireworks code and throwing flares all over the place. This can be very dangerous if they set fire to the flags they've also smuggled in.

Beside The Seaside

The Real Madrid faithful opted for a nautical theme on this massive flag unveiled at the Bernabeu at the end of the 2006–07 season before a clash with Real Mallorca, and luckily for the loyal home supporters, their title dreams didn't sink without a trace as Los Blancos pipped bitter rivals Barcelona to the title.

Pride Of Penarol

No football banner has ever come bigger or better than the whopping 16,400ft² (1524m²), two tonnes yellow and black beauty made by fans of Uruguayan giants Penarol in 2011. The flag took four months to make and the fans raised £25,000 for all the material they needed. Carried to the stadium by 300 volunteers, when the flag was unfurled at a Copa Libertadores clash against Independiente, it stretched almost halfway around the entire stadium.

Grass Burns

Groundsmen spend hours and hours lovingly grooming their grass so it's a safe bet the man in charge of the turf at the San Siro was less than impressed as fans littered his beautiful pitch with flares during a Milan derby in 2005. Inter's Juan Veron (far left) and Marco Materazzi and AC Milan's Rui Costa look on in shock and amazement.

Bring Your Own

Bayern Munich fans enjoyed an impromptu barbecue in the upper tier of the Allianz Arena with a barrage of flares before the 2012 Champions League final. But it proved the 'highlight' of the night for them as they lost a penalty shoot-out against Chelsea.

Now You See It...

It might look like the ball is on fire in this picture taken during the USA's clash with Honduras in Washington in 2001 but it's actually just a smoke bomb thrown onto the pitch. Honduras' Julio Cesar cunningly dribbles straight through the smoke to confuse America's Preki Radosvljevic, which is definitely a trick you won't find in the usual coaching manuals.

Put A Sock In It

Football and politics don't usually mix well, which Hapoel Tel Aviv star John Paintsil discovered during the 2006 World Cup finals when he scored for his native Ghana against the Czech Republic, reaching into his sock to reveal a small Israel flag that he stashed there before kick-off. "I love the fans in Israel," he explained after the game. "I just wanted to make them happy." The likes of FIFA however were far from happy at what they considered the player's political gesture and Paintsil was forced to make a series of apologies for his flag *faux pas*.

From Russia With Love

The 2012 European Championships in Poland and Ukraine were supposed to be one of the most security-conscious tournaments ever held, which makes it a complete mystery exactly how crafty Russian fans managed to smuggle in this simply enormous flag for their game with neighbours Poland in Warsaw. The unlucky fans hidden underneath the giant banner for most of the match probably failed to see much of the action or the funny side, though when they heard the crowd roar in appreciation at Poland's superb equaliser from the co-host nation's skipper Jakub Blaszczykowski, they probably felt a little less frustrated.

117

BLOW-UP FUN!

Football's great but some supporters are adamant that it's an even greater spectacle if you're waving a giant inflatable toy from the stands and judging by these examples, they might just be right...

Fantastic Fruit

The inflatable craze that swept British football in the late 1980s and early 1990s was a phenomenon which briefly threatened to leave thousands of fans gasping for breath and it all began when Manchester City faced West Brom in 1988. During the game, the waggish City fans began chanting for "Imre Banana" to come off the bench, even though his real name was Imre Varadi, but the nickname stuck and the City supporters decided to bring inflatable bananas to every game after that, paving the way for fans the length and breadth of the country to follow suit with their own array of comedy blow-ups.

Come Back!

Contrary to popular belief, that's not the smallest referee you've ever seen but rather an irritated Colombian official by the name of Jose Torres Cadena chasing a giant beachball that was thrown onto the pitch during Germany's 1994 World Cup quarter-final against Bulgaria, proving that size really is all relative. The pranksters who spent hours blowing up the giant beachball were easy to spot at Giants Stadium: they were the red-faced ones gasping for air. When the match resumed there were plenty more red faces, and gasps, but they were in surprise as Bulgaria won 2–1 against the embarrassed Germans to reach the semi-final.

Beachball Gaffe

As a general rule of thumb, inflatables should always remain with the supporters in the stands and the consequences of a stray blow-up drifting onto the pitch can be disastrous. And quite funny. One such unfortunate incident occurred during Sunderland's clash with Liverpool at the Stadium of Light in 2009 when an inflatable beachball smuggled in by the visiting fans was thrown onto the pitch just as Darren Bent unleashed a shot at goal. Sadly for Liverpool, the 'real' ball took a wicked deflection off the air-filled impostor, deceiving goalkeeper Pepe Reina and hitting the back of the net. Reds manager Rafa Benitez simply hit the roof.

Down Periscope!

The threat of relegation can do funny things to nervous fans but in the case of the Walsall faithful, it brought out a decidedly dry sense of humour as their team struggled out on the pitch. The Saddlers supporters decided comedy was the best way to deal with their precarious situation and took to taking inflatable submarines to matches, chanting a chorus of "going down, going down, going down" every time the team conceded a goal or lost a match.

Rock And A Hard Place

Bournemouth is another seaside club but the Cherries fans were dismayed when they unsuccessfully tried to place a bulk order of inflatable sticks of rock but were determined not to let the unforeseen setback spoil the party. The supporters put their heads together and agreed gigantic inflatable crayons looked a little like sticks of rock and so an unconventional but inventive south coast craze began.

Panther Prank

Cartoon characters make great inflatables but it remains a mystery exactly why Stoke City fans opted to start brandishing hundreds of Pink Panthers at their matches during their 1990–91 campaign. Rumour has it the club's commercial manager went to the nearest toy warehouse when the inflatable craze kicked off and could only get his hands on panthers but whatever the explanation, the Potters faithful looked pretty in pink for the rest of the season.

Happy Harry

Grimsby fans were quick to jump on the inflatable bandwagon and they ensured that their airy mascots had a local flavour, opting for a blow-up Harry the Haddock to reflect the town's fishing industry. Thousands of the four-foot-long fish were spotted at Mariners' games, offering countless chances for supporters to make jokes about getting 'battered' whenever the team lost.

Party People

Brazil is famous for the samba and pretty much anywhere and everywhere fans of the country's football team travel, you'll see them dancing. This particular example comes from the 2006 World Cup finals in Germany and took place before the start of the tournament, proving South American supporters really don't need any excuse at all for an impromptu party. And if Brazil were to go on to win the 2014 World Cup on home soil, the celebration party might just continue all the way through to the beginning of the 2018 tournament.

SHALL WE DANCE?

Football is meant to be a joyous celebration (particularly if your team happens to be winning), so it should come as no great surprise when some excitable fans get carried away and simply have to throw some shapes.

Dancing Dutch

The Dutch team has deservedly earned a great reputation for its stylish total football but judging by this colourful but slightly chaotic conga in the historic centre of Frankfurt during the 2006 World Cup, the team's supporters are sadly not quite as easy on the eye, or as well balanced. On the positive side, at least none of the fans fell into the fountain before kick-off. Sadly, on the negative side for the men in orange, the dancing ended prematurely with a 1–0 loss to Portugal in the last 16.

Picture Perfect

Type 'human jumbotron' into a well-known internet search engine and you will find the most amazing co-ordinated dance moves you've ever seen, courtesy of football fans in North Korea. Organised with military precision, more than one thousand supporters go through a series of complicated routines and costume changes to create pictures and messages for the rest of the crowd. The choreography is so stunning and the dancing so precise that you'll find it very hard to believe that you're watching a mass of people rather than a giant video screen.

Double Conga

Local rivalry was temporarily put to one side on the final day of the 2009–10 season when fans of Colchester United and Leyton Orient decided that a mass conga would be more entertaining than watching the match itself. Spotting that hundreds of Orient supporters had begun dancing in unison behind the goal at their end of the stadium, U's fans responded by dancing up and down their own aisles, a bizarre but entertaining example of two sets of supporters on exactly the same wavelength.

Strictly Skills

A new dance craze, 'Street Style' is a cool mash-up between break dancing and juggling a football in which two 'players' go head-to-head in front of a panel of eagle-eyed judges. Each competitor gets 20 seconds to impress with a mixture of moves and skills before passing the ball to their opponent. It's basically keepie-uppie on a dance floor and it's now so popular that there's even a World Series.

Silly Bhoys

Celebrating winning a title can do strange things to supporters and the dozen Celtic fans who saw their team wrap up the Scottish Premier League title in 2012 went absolutely nuts, dancing a jig slap bang in the middle of a busy dual carriageway, causing a traffic jam. The gang were so proud of their efforts that they posted the clips of their antics on Twitter, prompting the police to launch an investigation into the unusual cause of the congestion.

Manchester Mayhem

They say imitation is the sincerest form of flattery and Manchester City fans were seriously impressed when Poland's Lech Poznan visited Eastlands for a Europa League game in 2010. It wasn't the visitors' beautiful football that caught the City faithful's eye but rather their unique dance moves. The Poles repeatedly turned their back on the action, put their arms around each other and bounced up and down. City supporters immediately 'borrowed' the routine and the now famous 'Poznan' dance was born.

GET YOUR KIT ON!

Most sane supporters head to the big game with their clothes firmly on. There are however a minority of daring and sometimes dangerous fans who simply can't resist the temptation to strip off and streak across the pitch just when the players and stewards least expect it...

Festive Frolic

Christmas is traditionally a time to make merry and one female fan in the crowd for the North East derby between Middlesbrough and Newcastle in December 1998 was obviously very merry indeed, bursting onto the pitch wearing a sexy Santa suit, hat and boots and exposing her breasts to an amused Paul Gascoigne. Gazza admitted he'd thought Christmas had come early while the streaker made her excuses and headed back to the office party to find the nearest photocopier.

Pleased To Meet You

Many football streakers are more than happy just to break through the line of stewards by the side of the pitch and gallop on the grass like headless chickens but not the nude interloper who gatecrashed the Aston Villa versus Liverpool game in 1995 and dashed straight towards Andy Townsend. But rather than indulging in the usual tomfoolery, the streaker politely shook the Villa midfielder's hand before sprinting off in a vain attempt to escape the posse of stewards and policemen who were in hot pursuit.

Defenders are not always famed for their good looks but the female streaker who bounced onto the pitch at Hillsborough during Sheffield Wednesday's clash with Brighton in 2005 certainly believed beauty was in the eye of the beholder, running up to shocked Owls defender John Hills for a hug and kiss. Hills prayed his wife wasn't in the crowd while the streaker decided he wasn't really boyfriend material.

Stings Like A Bee

Streakers are like Marmite – you either love them or hate them and unfortunately for the foolish fella who decided to go al fresco at Burnley's 2002 game with Preston, Clarets mascot Bertie Bee was definitely not a fan. The streaker initially evaded the despairing lunge of an out-of-shape steward but just as he thought he had the Turf Moor pitch all to himself, Bertie came to the rescue and slammed the naked invader to the floor with a crunching rugby tackle to prove it's never wise to mess with a six-foot insect.

Kicking Off

Games between relegation-threatened teams are nervous affairs and fingernails were being chewed when Barnet met Torquay United at the end of the 2000-01 Third Division season. You could almost cut the tension at Underhill with a knife, so it wasn't the best time for a streaker to interrupt the action by waggling his bits around.

Final Flop

A serial stripping offender, Englishman Mark Roberts has got naked at hundreds of big sporting events over the years including the Ashes and American football's Super Bowl, but perhaps his most famous streak was at the 2003 UEFA Cup final between Celtic and Porto in Spain. Stealing the ball inside the Celtic half, Roberts dribbled past stunned defenders and raced towards the Porto goal but his weak shot failed to beat keeper Vitor Baia and to add insult to injury, he was immediately and violently bundled to the ground by three very angry policemen.

FRINGE FOOTBALL

Football is now played in shiny stadiums, on pristine pitches with 22 well-manicured players, watched by thousands of fans. But it hasn't always been so perfect. No one knows exactly where or when the game was born, but there are many historical and often crazy sports that bear more than a passing resemblance to modern football. From the violent Shrove Tuesday Ball Game to the ancient Chinese sport of *Cuju*, they're sports that don't pull any punches.

Competitors get down and dirty in the mud during the annual Swamp Football World Championships in Finland.

FOOTBALL IN THE STICKS

The professional game may boast the glitz and the glamour (and mountains of money) but that's not to say village football doesn't produce its fair share of drama and bizarre tales, proving bigger doesn't always mean better.

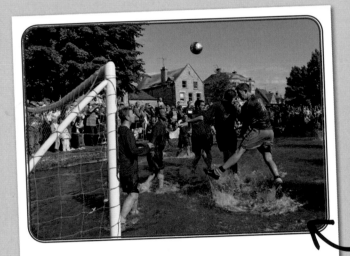

Water On The Pitch

The right choice of footwear for a match can be crucial and for players of the Bourton-on-the-Water team in the Cotswolds it probably should be Wellington rather than football boots. That's because for the past 70 years, Bourton have played their home games on the Windrush River in the village rather than a traditional grass-covered surface, with the goals set up under two bridges that span the three-metre-wide stream. Thankfully the water is only knee high, meaning players are in more danger of getting booked for diving than they are of drowning.

Madron Massacred

Enjoyment is the name of the game when it comes to village football but it's a safe bet the hapless players of Cornish side Madron didn't enjoy themselves in 2010 when they found themselves on the wrong end of an eye-watering 55–0 scoreline against Illogan. The fact it was actually the Illogan reserve team only rubbed salt into the wound while Madron didn't do themselves any favours when they turned up for the game with just seven players. "I know everybody is probably laughing at us," admitted club secretary Alan Davenport after the team's nightmare 90 minutes, "but we will battle on."

The Italian Job

Village sides rarely enjoy the luxury of playing abroad but West Auckland were the exception to the rule back in 1909 when they unexpectedly found themselves playing the mighty Juventus in Italy. The County Durham team were invited to Turin to compete in the inaugural Sir Thomas Lipton trophy because the English Football Association had refused to send an XI and against all the odds, the West Auckland side made up of amateurs and miners thrashed Juventus 6–1 in the final, proving once again that David really can overcome Goliath.

Outrageous OAP

Countless village teams have produced their own calendars in a bid to boost their club coffers but none of them was surely as eye-catching as Ancaster Athletic's 2008 effort, which featured a naked appearance from 102-year-old Nora Hardwick. 'Miss November' decided to strip off after living in the Lincolnshire village for more than 70 years but insisted her contribution was as 'artistic' as possible. "It was all very tastefully done," Nora said. "You couldn't see any of the bits or anything. I suppose they asked me because I'm the oldest person in the village and it's just a bit of fun really."

What's In A Name?

It's not unusual for a couple of players in the same team to share a surname even if they're not related but the name game got seriously out of hand in 2012 at Bungay FC in Suffolk when all 22 players on show (not to mention the referee, linesmen, substitutes and even the mascots) were called Bungay. The bizarre game was the brainchild of club official Shaun Cole who invited Bungays from Britain, as well as America and Australia, to take part in the charity match which made a mockery of the referee writing down anyone's name in his book. "It is a brilliant way of putting Bungay on the map," Cole said. "I thought the idea for the match was nuts when it was first suggested and it is still nuts today."

Tree Hazard

The sunshine in Brazil can be seriously energy-sapping but back in the 1990s any team playing on this bizarre pitch in the rural region of Brazil could find a bit of very welcome shade under a handily placed tree. It may have proved an unusual obstacle, especially for visiting sides who weren't accustomed to playing one-twos with a tree, but at least neither team was ever short of half-time oranges.

Messi Madness

Any team in the world would love to have Argentina star Lionel Messi in their ranks and in 2011 the deluded chairman of French village side FC Borne thought he'd try his luck and actually ask to sign the Barcelona goal machine. After one too many glasses of wine on a night out with friends, Borne's Cedric Enjolras submitted a formal request to Barça for Messi's signature but his drunken message was intercepted by the French FA, who failed to see the funny side and immediately suspended the comedy chairman for six months.

Internet Entrepreneurs

Sponsorship is the lifeblood of many cash-strapped non-league clubs and Scottish team Blackburn United decided they'd cast their net as wide as possible in 2012 when they went looking for a new sugar daddy – selling their sponsorship rights on eBay. The West Lothian outfit asked for a modest £800 from companies to get their logo on the players' shirts for a season but were disappointed when the only replies they received were emails offering unbelievable discounts on iPads.

Tribal Ties

There's roughly 10,000 miles between the Lancashire village of Clitheroe and the Australian Outback but in 2002 distance proved no barrier to a bizarre football story when a tribe of Aborigines agreed to sponsor the local team. The deal was struck after lifelong Clitheroe FC fan Bruce Dowles spent four months living with the Aborigines and on returning to the UK, he persuaded them to stump up £125 for an advert in the club's matchday programme highlighting their plight Down Under. In return, the Clitheroe players ran out onto the pitch to the sound of a didgeridoo, much to the bemusement of the 105 fans who turned up for the game, while the Aboriginal flag was flown above the clubhouse.

Giant's Game

According to legend elephants never forget but this jumbo duo clearly didn't remember their shin pads at the Surin Elephant Round-Up Festival in Thailand, an annual opportunity for the big guys to showcase their footballing skills. Standing on the ball is discouraged while it's an automatic red card and an early bath for any elephant sneakily attempting to trip an opponent with their trunk.

Cold Comfort

It's an annual tradition for local residents in Shenyang in China to go for a swim in a frozen river at Christmas time, but before taking their dip, the hardy souls like to warm up with a quick kick-about on the ice. It's great for sliding tackles but someone really should tell them you don't play the beautiful game with a basketball.

Football Faith

Some people say football is a religion and in the summer of 2010 the Reverend Nick Shutt decided to bring the beautiful game and the Church even closer together when he decided to re-create Leonardo da Vinci's famous 'Last Supper' painting using the players from his local village team. Devon-based Reverend Shutt asked the Walkhampton FC team to pose for his unusual religious re-creation in their full kit inside the clubhouse, quietly promising the players the 'Big Man' would 'do them a favour' in their next match. "I am creating a series of classical art work that fits in with twentieth-century life," Shutt explained. "I thought that re-creating it with footballers could get an ancient message across using up-to-date imagery and it's particularly relevant during the World Cup."

Dynamite Danger

Village pitches are often infamous for poor playing surfaces but in 1956 the turf of Harbertonford FC in Devon took a serious and sudden turn for the worse when a huge brick chimney crashed onto the half-way line. The chimney was part of a nearby mill which was dynamited by demolition experts but they got the calculations horribly wrong.

Aerial Bombardment

Basically an early Japanese version of keepie-uppie, 'Kemari' is nearly 1,500 years old and involves a team of players repeatedly heading, kicking and even elbowing a small sphere in a desperate bid to stop it hitting the floor. The ball, called the Mari, was traditionally made from deerskin and was probably the inspiration for the modern hacky sack.

BACK TO MY ROOTS

The beautiful game as we know it has been entertaining the masses for around 150 years but the history of the sport goes back much, much further – as these weird and wonderful examples of early versions of football go to prove...

North Of The Border

The good folk of the Scottish village of Scone used to play an interesting version of 'mob football' centuries ago, fielding a team of married men against a side of carefree bachelors. The 'husbands' had to get the ball into a small pot that was placed on nearby hills while the fellas who'd never walked up the aisle were tasked with dipping the ball in the local river. The team with the most 'points' was declared the winner although it was usually the bachelors who were triumphant because the married players had to reluctantly knock off early to help their other halves with the housework.

No Murders Please!

The slightly insane residents of Atherstone in Warwickshire have been playing their traditional 'Shrove Tuesday Ball Game' for centuries and there's only one rule – players cannot kill each other. There are no teams and no goals and the aim is to be the one holding the heavy leather ball at the end of all the wrestling, kicking and general, violent mayhem. The game celebrated its 800th anniversary in 1999 and usually kicks off at 3.00pm and lasts for a couple of hours, although the battered and bruised villagers tend to be nursing their injuries for weeks after the final whistle.

Calcio Kicks

Created in the Italian city of Florence over 500 years ago, 'Calcio Fiorentino' ('Florentine kick game') is still played today and if you've got a giant sand pit, 54 players (27 per team), eight referees and a spare 50 minutes, you could have a match. Diego Maradona would be good at this game because players can use their feet and hands and goals are scored by throwing the ball over a marked spot on the perimeter of the square pitch. Worryingly, head-butting, choking and punching are all legal but they do draw the line at kicks to the head.

Sport Of Emperors

Legend has it that a Chinese Emperor by the name of Huangdi came up with the game called 'Cuju' around 4,500 years ago as a way of preparing his soldiers for battle but it remains something of a mystery how a sport in which the players kicked a ball to each other actually helped to win any wars. Unlike modern football, the aim of Cuju was not to score goals but score the most points, with points deducted from the 12 to 16 players on each side for both short and over-hit passes, as well as kicking the ball out of play.

Eton Antics

The complete laws of the famous 'Eton Field Game' would give a rocket scientist a headache but to try and cut a very long story short, it's a 200-year-old sport devised by Eton School that mixes a bit of football and rugby. Teams can score a goal for three points by hitting the back of the opposition net but there's five points on offer if they can score a 'rogue' by booting the ball off an opposition player and deflecting it over their goal line at one end of the pitch. A player then has to touch the ball to complete the 'rogue' and avoid getting a detention from the PE teacher.

133

Foot Up

Football's answer to volleyball, 'Sepak Takraw' is a popular game in Malaysia and Thailand that dates back 600 years and although you'll need a net to play, there are definitely no goalkeepers. The sport sees two teams of three players line up on a pitch roughly the same size as a badminton court and kick, volley and head a small ball over a 1.5-metre net. With points and sets, the scoring system is similar to tennis but with much less grunting and fewer arguments with the umpires.

Toilet Target

Going to the gents got a bit more exciting in 2007 when a German company unveiled the Klo-Kicker, a miniature goal that sat inside a urinal, encouraging men to aim for the back of the net when nature called. The tiny football changed colour from red to white if you were accurate with your 'shot', though plans to organise a lavatory-inspired World Cup remained unrealised on the grounds of decency and public hygiene.

Girl Power

Table football – known as foosball in some parts of the world – was invented by an Englishman by the name of Harold Searles Thornton in the 1920s and it has proved to be hugely popular with many generations of football lovers around the world. Even if the advent of computerised games has lessened their appeal, there are still local and national table football championships. However, in 2009 table football was given a serious makeover when designers decided to replace the iconic players with rows of Barbie dolls. The new figures certainly look pretty in pink but whether table football and high heels are the ideal combination remains a talking point.

GAMES AND PASTIMES

Football doesn't necessarily have to be played on a pitch and as these examples prove, as long as our love of the beautiful game continues, there will be a market for all manner of spin-offs, simulations and silliness.

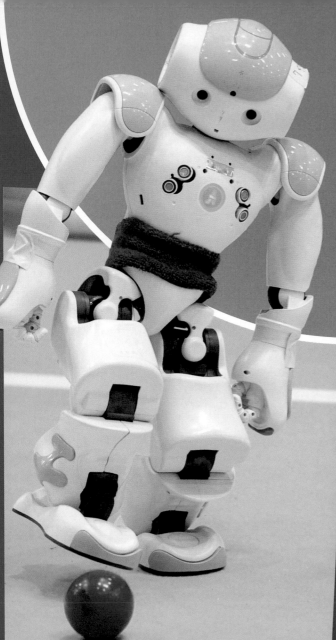

Mechanical Madness

Some scientists dream of a future in which robots are able to do anything humans can and the creators of this automaton, in action at the 2011 Robo Cup in Turkey, decided they'd have a stab at building a goalkeeper with artificial intelligence. A pity then that no one told the designers of the robotic custodian that intelligence – artificial or otherwise – isn't always a prerequisite for those who go between the sticks.

Business Of The Board

The first edition of 'Monopoly' went on sale in America in 1934 and these days there are several special football editions of the iconic board game. One of the most recent was the official FIFA version released ahead of the 2010 World Cup in South Africa with the 32 countries in the finals replacing the traditional property squares on the board and stadiums standing in for the railway stations. England's early exit from the tournament, however, really didn't help sales of the game in the UK.

Shankly's Subbuteo

Legend has it that Liverpool manager Bill Shankly once used a Subbuteo set to illustrate a team talk before his team faced arch-rivals Manchester United and this picture proves the Anfield icon was definitely a fan of the classic game. Shankly claimed three First Division titles as Liverpool boss but as far as we know he never won any Subbuteo silverware.

Game Plan

Sending scouts all over the world to watch players is an expensive business so, in 2008, Premier League side Everton decided to save themselves cash by signing a deal with the makers of 'Football Manager'. It gave the club exclusive access to a database of more than 370,000 players in 50 countries, with the aim of identifying the best unknown and obscure players in the game and only then despatch scouts to actually watch them in action. This was fine until the Everton staff became addicted to the simulation game and they refused to stop playing until they'd taken Leyton Orient to the top of the Premier League.

EXTREME KEEPIE-UPPIE

Irate coaches can often be overheard screaming "get it on the deck" at their players but as these mind-blowing examples prove, some people are simply born to keep the football in the air.

Head Case

Balancing the ball on your head is a tricky talent that eludes most of us but Bangladesh's Abdul Halim has perfected the technique and in 2011 he set a new world record for walking while balancing a football on his bonce. Halim covered 9.4 miles at the National Stadium in Dhaka with the ball on his cranium and once officials had confirmed he hadn't actually stuck the ball on with superglue, he was hailed as the new record holder.

Car Craziness

Some keepie-uppie records are more bizarre than others, and the mind-blowing milestone set by Kosovo's Agim Agushi in 2004 was absolutely bonkers. Agushi drove seven kilometres in a car with the roof open while heading a football. It is fair to assume that he spent the journey thanking his lucky stars that all the traffic lights were green and there wasn't a policeman in sight as he completed his unusual challenge.

Coordinated Capers

There are a lot of people in China and in 2010, exactly 1,062 of them got together to set a new world record for the most people simultaneously doing keepie-uppie. However, if you look closely at the picture (far right, third player down), the young chap clearly holding his football rather than juggling with it is not following the same script as the rest of the crowd.

Marathon Man

The 26 miles of a London marathon are the ultimate test of athletic endurance but back in 2011 England's John Farnworth decided to make the race even more of a challenge by juggling a football the entire distance of the course. Once doctors had established that Farnworth was not in fact clinically insane, he was allowed to embark on his kamikaze keepie-uppie mission and finished the race in an impressive 12 hours and 15 minutes.

Horizontal Hero

Doing keepie-uppies can be a tiring business, which is perhaps why England's Daniel Bolt decided to try and set a new world record for keeping the ball in the air – while lying on his back. Once Bolt had got nice and comfy in 2008, he set about his task and recorded a record time of 21 minutes and 14 seconds before he accidentally nodded off.

Awesome Ash

Speed was definitely the name of the game for Ash Randall in 2010 when he tried to set the record for the most touches of a ball in one minute with just the soles of his feet. The Cardiff City fan embarked on his attempt during half-time of the Bluebirds' league game with Watford and was all smiles after 60 action-packed seconds with a new world record of 220 keepie-uppies.

African Assault

It takes imagination to think of new and innovative keepie-uppie records and Swiss Paul Sahli definitely had his thinking cap on when he pondered exactly how many steps of a ladder he could climb while juggling a football. The only way to find out was to grab the nearest ladder and ball and give it a whirl with Sahli eventually managing to climb 111 steps before vertigo got the better of him.

Streets of London

Dan Magness must be addicted to keepie-uppie and not content with setting the record for the longest time keeping the ball airborne, he's also the record holder for the longest distance covered while juggling the ball. In 2010, the incredible Englishman started at Fulham's Craven Cottage ground and finished at Tottenham's White Hart Lane to set his magical milestone, covering an unbelievable 36 miles of the streets of London without once letting the ball hit the pavement.

AND FINALLY...

Modern footballers are as big a part of popular culture as *X Factor* or Facebook and football is no longer only about what happens on the pitch. In fact, we seem to be more obsessed with what they do when they're not kicking a ball about. Here's a selection of players' best and worst of choices of weird wheels, dire decisions to move into the worlds of ads, music and acting and some of their other halves who don't conform to today's image of a WAG.

Hundreds of thousands of fans line the streets of Madrid for the open-top bus celebration after Spain's victory at Euro 2012.

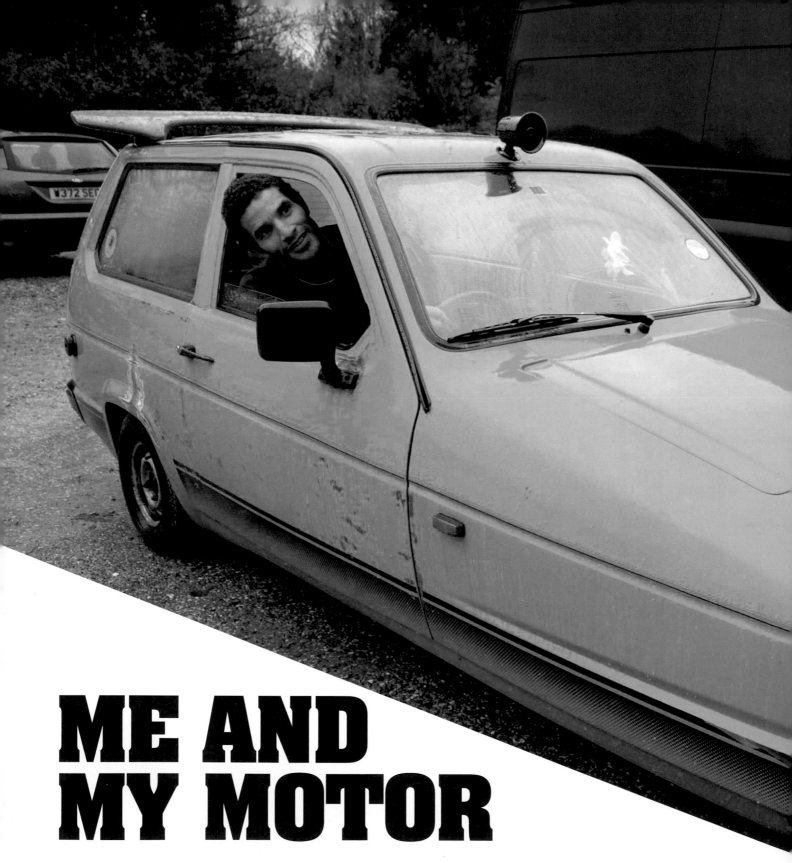

CHAPTER 8

ME AND MY MOTOR

Footballers absolutely love cars and most training ground car parks these days are bursting at the seams with top-of-the-range BMWs and Ferraris, Porsches and Audis. But that's not to say every modern player always opts for such obvious, stylish and expensive ways of getting from A to B.

Three-Wheel Woe

When he was modelling for fashion house Armani, David James was a picture of elegance and style, but the England goalkeeper looked anything but cool back in 2008 when he was forced to drive home from the Portsmouth training ground in a blue Robin Reliant. Complete with a totally unnecessary rear spoiler and speaker system playing farmyard animal noises, James had to take to the roads in the embarrassing three-wheeler as a forfeit after his team-mates decided he put in the worst performance in training.

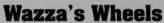

Wazza's Wheels

After finding fame and fortune with Manchester United and England, Wayne Rooney now needs a garage the size of an aircraft hangar to house his massive collection of cool cars, but when he was a youngster with Everton in 2003 and he got his driving licence, his first ride was a blue Ford SportKa. "I'm looking forward to driving myself to training in my new car," Rooney said after sacking his chauffeur. "It's just a huge relief to have passed my test."

Green Machine

In his heyday, Gary Neville rarely took prisoners as part of the Manchester United or England back four but he did show a more caring and environmentally conscious side to his personality in 2009 when he splashed out £20,000 on an eco-friendly Toyota Prius. The Old Trafford star plumped for a white model of the ultra-efficient Japanese motor and promptly began lecturing his bemused United team-mates about miles per gallon and their carbon emissions.

Tight Squeeze

Didier Drogba is what's known in the business as a 'big unit' but the six-foot-three Chelsea striker opted for something altogether smaller when it came to his choice of wheels, buying a compact Mini Cooper S Works to help him negotiate the notorious London traffic. Quite how the big Ivory Coast forward managed to squeeze in to his modest Mini remains a mystery.

Free Car

Most players treasure their cars as if they were part of the family but Birmingham midfielder Olivier Kapo bucked the trend in 2008 when he gave his £30,000 Mercedes to one of the club's youth players. The lucky youngster was James McPike, who had asked Kapo for a pair of his boots as a souvenir at the end of the season, but instead of giving him his muddy footwear, the generous Frenchman handed his car keys to the stunned but very grateful 20-year-old.

Bright Spark

One of the first rules for footballers buying a car is the fewer miles to the gallon it does the better but no one told Chelsea midfielder Florent Malouda before he opted to get behind the wheel of an electric Tesla Roadster. "The other players were asking questions about the 'funny' car," admitted Malouda. "I explained the performance and when you drive it is like a normal sports car but when you switch on the engine it is really silent, so it impresses everyone." An endorsement which had absolutely nothing whatsoever to do with Malouda's sponsorship deal with Tesla.

Economical Eto'o

Cameroon superstar Samuel Eto'o has earned millions in a glittering career in European football but the striker still decided to watch the pennies when he took wife Georgette on holiday to Greece in 2007, hiring a scruffy Fiat Scudo people carrier rather than opting for the chauffeur-driven limo which he could have easily afforded. At least there was plenty of room in the back for the suitcases.

Pretty In Pink?

No one could ever accuse Republic of Ireland midfielder Stephen Ireland of being the shy and retiring type but there was a good reason why he lived up to his reputation as one of the game's showmen. In 2008, he turned up for a Manchester City training session in a £90,000 black Range Rover, complete with customised pink alloy wheels, grille and seats. But it was not done to satisfy his ego, or to show off to City team-mates; Ireland had paid big money to help the breast cancer awareness charity campaign.

The Original Playboy

Believe it or not, footballers were not always as rich or famous as they are today, but legendary Northern Irishman George Best changed all that. In the 1960s and 70s, he made front-page headlines with his flamboyant lifestyle off the pitch, as much as dominating the back pages with his sublime skill on it. Dubbed 'Gorgeous George' by his army of fanatical female fans, the Manchester United icon lived the dream, splashing his cash on luxury items such as this state-of-the-art Jaguar.

Silly Cisse

Most of the motors in your average Premier League, Serie A or La Liga car park are European but players really wanting to stand out from the crowd import their wheels from America. Cue France striker Dijribil Cisse, who shipped over an eye-catching Plymouth Prowler, complete with Hot Rod-style front wheels. Car makers Chrysler only manufactured the Prowler for four years but Cisse still managed to get his hands on one before everyone saw sense and closed the factory.

Smart Move

It often seems footballers are locked in a constant battle to see who can drive the most outrageously oversized car possible but Tottenham defender Benoit Assou-Ekotto decided to go in the opposite direction when he bought himself a dinky, two-seater Smart Car rather than a gigantic, gas-guzzling motor. The Spurs star only realised his terrible mistake when he tried and failed to fit his famous afro into his new micro motor.

Which Side Are You On?

Tottenham caused quite a stir in 1994 when they announced the signing of German star Jürgen Klinsmann. To help him adapt to his new life in London, the striker shipped this left-hand-drive, convertible VW Beetle over with him. Spurs, of course, warned their new signing that opportunities to lower his sunroof would be few and far between because of the weather, but Klinsmann was far more shocked when he realised that everyone in England drove on the wrong side of the road.

Jenny's Job

Republic of Ireland striker Kevin Doyle tied the knot with childhood sweetheart Jenny Harney in the summer of 2010 and the couple can always fall back on Jenny's skills as an industrial engineer if Kevin's football career ever takes an unexpected turn for the worse.

Caroline's Castle

Some WAGs admit it's the size of a footballer's pay packet that gets them going but no one could accuse Caroline Luel-Brockdorff of thinking that way when she got together with Denmark striker Nicklas Bendtner. A member of the Danish Royal Family, Caroline is a baroness and owns her own castle, while her £400 million personal fortune puts Bendtner's more "modest" £2.5 million annual income seriously in the shade.

WONDERFUL WAGS

With a reputation for serious shopping and a fixation with fashion, football's new generation of WAGs have not enjoyed the best of publicity in recent years. But that doesn't mean all of the game's 'other halves' simply spend their time watching hubby charging around the pitch.

Caring Kuyt

Many WAGs quit their jobs when they tie the knot but Gertrude Kuyt proved an exception to the rule when she got hitched to Dutch star Dirk. The childhood sweethearts certainly weren't short of cash but Gertrude decided to shun the celebrity lifestyle and continued to work as a nurse at a care home, only hanging up her uniform when the couple's second child was born. She also helped set up the Dirk Kuyt Foundation, a charity to help disadvantaged children in Holland and the Third World, deservedly earning Gertrude the title of one of football's most wonderful wives.

Student Days

English football was flabbergasted when Sven-Goran Eriksson selected a 17-year-old Theo Walcott for the 2006 World Cup finals but Walcott's girlfriend Melanie Slade didn't let the shock news upset her own plans. Slade was in the middle of her sixth-form studies at the time and a year after Theo's sudden fame, she passed A-Levels in Maths, Psychology and Biology. She went on to study physiotherapy at the University of London, which certainly came in handy as Walcott began picking up injuries faster than one of his trademark dashes down the right wing.

Pole To Pole

Arsenal goalkeeper Wojciech Szczesny needs to show plenty of athleticism between the sticks at the Emirates, which is probably why he was so smitten by fellow Pole Sandra Dziwiszek when the couple met at a party in Warsaw back in 2008. Dziwiszek is a Polish pole vaulter who has represented her country, while Szczesny is also a Polish international, meaning the couple are never poles apart when it comes to dinner conversation.

A Head For Business

When Manchester United and England star Michael Carrick got hitched to Lisa Roughhead in 2007, the midfielder didn't so much gain a wife as someone who could help him manage his sizeable salary. As well as being a qualified pilates instructor, Mrs Carrick also boasts a business degree, making her the perfect partner for a man with money to invest.

Roving Reporter

There's an old saying, 'if you can't beat them, join them', and it was advice that Sara Carbonero took literally when her other half, Iker Casillas, jetted off to South Africa with the Spain team for the 2010 World Cup. Carbonero followed him to the tournament to work as a pitch-side reporter for Spanish TV rather than going shopping with the other WAGs but the trip didn't exactly go to plan after she was accused of distracting Casillas in the warm-up before Spain's group stage game with Switzerland in Durban, presenting a preview piece to camera right behind his goal. Spain were beaten 1–0 by the Swiss but luckily for Carbonero, the team did eventually lift the World Cup.

Gospel Glory

It is not unusual for players to hook up with pop stars but sometimes the lady's musical tendencies only emerge after tying the knot, which was the case when Brazil's Kaka married Caroline Celico. Mrs Kaka had never been anywhere near a recording studio but after belting out a few tunes in the shower, she decided to release a 12-track gospel album which, to her credit, she wrote herself. Caroline decided to keep it in the family on her recording debut with the CD featuring songs dedicated to her hubby and another to their son Luca.

TV Talent

The *Match of the Day* sofa in England may still be waiting for its first female presenter but over in Europe, the ladies are welcomed with open arms on football shows. One such presenter is Alessia Ventura in Italy, who co-hosts a Sunday-evening programme called *Controcampo* and also happens to be dating AC Milan striker Filippio Inzaghi, which probably means the couple don't have to fight over the remote control when *X-Factor* is on at the same time as the big match.

Double Figures

Young footballers often sacrifice their studies in favour of honing their skills but that doesn't mean their other halves are not academically minded, as proven by Coleen Rooney who has 10 GCSEs to her name. Coleen and Wayne started seeing each other as teenagers but that didn't stop her doing her homework every night and getting four A grades.

Fitness First

Footballers need to look after their bodies to ensure they're ready for 90 minutes of action on Saturday afternoon, so it was probably a logical step for Phil Neville's wife Julie to try her hand as an internet entrepreneur selling organic foods and fitness supplements. Whether hubby Phil was ever brave enough to taste one of her green 'health' shakes is a secret the Nevilles have kept to themselves.

Rain Or Shine

The fickle British weather is notoriously difficult to predict but at least Arsenal midfielder Tomas Rosicky should never get caught out by the elements at training – his long-term partner Radka Kocurova used to work as a television weather girl in her native Czech Republic before relocating to London with him. Whether Tomas dared to warn her just how often it rains in England is unclear.

Clever Claudine

Dubbed the Republic of Ireland's answer to Posh and Becks, Robbie and Claudine Keane got married in the summer of 2008. She's a former winner of the Miss Ireland competition but Mrs Keane has brains as well as beauty and boasts a first-class honours degree in economics and mathematics from University College Dublin, proving once again that you should never judge a book by its rather attractive cover.

Rhyme Time

WAGs are not the exclusive preserve of Premier League footballers and Woking midfielder Paolo Vernazza hit the headlines in 2008 when he began dating the lovely Sapphira O'Shannon. There was nothing unusual in O'Shannon's part-time career as glamour model but she did successfully buck the WAG trend somewhat when it emerged she was also a self-published poet, although she struggled to come up with a decent ode to the beautiful game when she realised nothing really rhymed with 'technical area'.

147

Wonder Of Waddle

The king of the mullet, Chris Waddle reached number 20 in the UK charts in 1987 when he released the infamous 'Diamond Lights' with Spurs team-mate Glenn Hoddle, but the warbling winger had a second stab at pop stardom in France after he signed for Marseille in 1989, recording 'We've Got a Feeling' with team-mate Basil Boli. Cartoon zebras and the Houses of Parliament featured heavily in the Anglo-French-themed video but exactly what feeling the two players were having remains unclear.

Language Barrier

When he's not going on strike, sulking or demanding yet another transfer, Argentina striker Carlos Tevez likes to get together with his brother Diego and front up their band called Piola Vago. The group's biggest hit – 'Lose Control' – charted in Argentina but the grumpy forward admitted he doesn't bother to share his Spanish tunes with English team-mates. "Here it's all hip-hop, all in English, so they don't understand a thing," he said. "They want to hear it, they ask me but I say no to them."

TOP OF THE POPS

Footballers' attempts at singing are usually limited to a crack at karaoke at the club Christmas party but unfortunately some misguided players become convinced their talents deserve a wider audience and insist on actually releasing records.

Roque Rocks

Some players' involvement in recording a song can be very brief indeed and they don't come any briefer than Roque Santa Cruz's contribution to 2004 heavy metal tune 'Ich Roque', written by German group Sportfreunde Stiller. All the Paraguay striker had to do was say "Ich Roque" ("I Rock") at the start of the chorus and leave the rest of the work to the band for one of the most one-sided musical collaborations ever. Which is probably why the group decided to film the video for the song in a deserted DIY store.

Musical Morte

With his bleached blonde hair and youthful good looks, Norwegian midfielder Morte Ganst Pedersen always had the look of a member of a boy band about him and after years of jokes about his 'look' he decided to call everyone's bluff... and actually join a boy band. Teaming up with professionals from the Norwegian Premier League, Pedersen became part of a group that after literally days of debate decided to call themselves The Players and released a track called 'This is for Real'. And it really was, as the song became a big hit across Scandinavia.

Bum Rap

Plenty of players have a nickname in the dressing room but USA striker Clint Dempsey decided to adopt the alias of 'Deuce' when he recorded a single for Nike in the build-up to the 2006 World Cup in Germany. Performing alongside XO and Big Hawk, Dempsey rapped his heart out on the song 'Don't Tread' but the song failed to inspire the American team as they headed home early after failing to win any of their group stage games at the tournament.

Bonkers Ballad

It's fair to say 1979 was a vintage year for Kevin Keegan. The England striker won the Bundesliga title with Hamburg and he was voted European Footballer of the Year, so it really was a shame that he had to undo all his good work by releasing his awful single 'Head Over Heels in Love' in the same year. A toe-curling ballad that saw KK warbling away in the biggest flares in the history of fashion and an enormous shirt collar, the tune amazingly hung around the charts for six full weeks. Which absolutely no one was head over heels about.

I Can't Dance

These days Holland legend Ruud Gullit sports a very sensible short haircut but back in his playing days he was famous for his flowing dreadlocks, so it was probably inevitable his first foray into music would be with a reggae track. Gullit's tune 'Not the Dancing Kind' was released in 1984 and was a modest hit, but Bob Marley it was not.

Big Bad Vinnie

Midfield-hardman-turned-Hollywood-star Vinnie Jones has enjoyed great success in his post-football career as an actor but the same couldn't be said of his foray into pop. The former Wimbledon and Wales player appeared on the BBC's *Top of the Pops* in 2002 to perform his cover version of 1970s classic 'Big Bad Leroy Brown' but his performance failed to wow the viewers and Jones wisely decided acting rather than crooning was his forte.

Misleading Title

Back in 1999 Andy Cole was at the peak of his footballing powers, banging in the goals for Manchester United and lifting the Champions League trophy, and it probably seemed the perfect time for the England striker to have a dabble in the music business. Cue the release of his R'n'B single 'Outstanding' but sadly for the United star his effort proved to be anything but outstanding and after reaching a lowly number 68 in its first week on sale, the single sank without a trace and Cole reluctantly went back to kicking a ball about for a living.

Light Entertainment

The Matrix was the big blockbuster of 1999 and its groundbreaking special effects were obviously a big influence on the video for Youri Djorkaeff's single 'Vivre Dans Ta Lumière' ('Live in the Light') which was released the following year. Fresh from helping France win Euro 2000, Djorkaeff went for the leather trouser and vest look for the video and once the clever chaps with computers had got their hands on the footage, the world was presented with a headache-inducing three-and-a-half minutes' worth of Youri inexplicably appearing and disappearing from view.

Cruyff's Cringe

Dutch legend Johan Cruyff is famous for the legendary 'turn' he invented and which is still named after him. He's not famous however for his singing career which began (and thankfully ended) in 1969, and if you're ever unlucky enough to hear his single – 'Oei Oei Oei (Dat Was Me Weer een Loei)' – you'll know exactly why. The oom-pah-style song is truly terrible and if you listen very, very carefully, you can almost hear Cruyff dying of embarrassment as the band plays on.

Savage Slaven

Croatia's Slaven Bilic was known as a tough and temperamental defender in his playing days with West Ham, Everton and Hajduk Split so it came as no surprise when he joined a band called Rawbau, who recorded a song called 'Atreno Ludil' ('Fiery Madness'). Bilic played rhythm guitar on the single, which the rockers released to coincide with the 2008 European Championships, and the patriotic Croatian public thought it was anything but madness as the song went straight to number one.

Wheels Of Steel

Many footballers have tried their luck as DJs but flamboyant French striker Djibril Cisse reckoned he was so good on the wheels of steel that he decided to release his own CD mix of his favourite dance tunes in 2008. Entitled *Music and Me: The DJ Inside Me*, the album featured a track called 'Got to Get Away', which probably struck a chord with supporters of any of the seven different clubs he's played for.

Wright Gets it All Wrong

Dancing in public, let alone in front of the cameras, is a risky business and former Arsenal and England striker Ian Wright should have definitely heeded the warning before he decided to make a complete fool of himself and advertise cooking sauce *Chicken Tonight*. Getting dressed up in a smoking jacket and cravat was bad enough but Wright's bizarre, jerky knees-and-elbow dance halfway through the TV advert made the audience desperately reach for the remote.

ADVERT FOR THE GAME

Some players yearn for something other than football, a life more adventurous (and even more lucrative) than simply kicking a ball around a pitch for 90 minutes. Sadly this often leads them into the world of advertising with frequently hilarious and embarrassing results.

Crunchy Kickabout

One of the golden rules of advertising is that a footballer must be shown showcasing their skills – no matter what they're promoting. Cue an embarrassed-looking Nicolas Anelka, Dirk Kuyt, Cesc Fabregas and Peter Crouch kicking around an empty tin of 'Pringles' in a 2010 TV ad which proved once and for all, footballers really can be used to sell absolutely anything as long as the price is right.

Crispy Keane

Roy Keane's opponents were more likely to be left with a flesh wound rather than a smile on their face after doing battle with the tough-tackling Manchester United midfielder but the Old Trafford bruiser briefly cast off his hard-man image in 2000 when he agreed to dress up as a cheeky multi-coloured leprechaun for a Walkers crisp advert. Not for the first or last time in his colourful career, the Republic of Ireland star had everyone in stitches.

The Shower Scene

Famed for his tight bubble perm and celebrity lifestyle, Kevin Keegan was something of a trailblazer as a player in the 1970s and 1980s but probably blazed just a bit too much of a trail when he appeared in an advert for Brut aftershave with heavyweight boxer Henry Cooper. The commercial featured the two greats enjoying a workout but things got a little steamy when they retreated to the shower to joke about who liked the manly smell of Brut the best. Things really bottomed out when Cooper removed his towel to throw at cheeky Kev.

ve Life
To the Fullest

Pelé

One in three men ove 40 years experience e   blems that interfere   ve life.

Men with ED report   less happy and emotionally satisfie   relationship

Chemical Cash

There aren't many men who would happily admit to even their closest friends that they needed 'help' in, ahem, the trouser department but most men aren't Pele, who became the face of Viagra in 2005. The Brazil legend told anyone who'd listen about the wonders of the drug, banking millions in the process while slightly less embarrassed men of a certain age suddenly rushed to their local chemists.

Dog Days

Some players advertise top-of-the range menswear, luxury scents or ridiculously expensive watches. Some aren't quite so lucky and Fernando Torres fell into that category after he agreed to appear in a truly awful TV advert for a dog-training school in his native Spain. Torres made a right dogs' dinner of the acting and most people agreed he was upstaged by a rather talented Alsatian.

Copy Cat

The worlds of football and office equipment don't have much in common, so why photocopier manufacturer Konika thought Brazilian superstar Ronaldinho would help them shift more machines in Japan remains a mystery. The absolutely awful 2007 advert featured the Samba star performing a series of tricks and playing a drum kit before a closing shot of the photocopier itself.

Lottery Losers

Back in the days when Chelsea defender Ashley Cole and his ex Cheryl were happily married they were seriously hot property and they decided to cash in on their marital fame in 2006 by appearing in an advert for the National Lottery wearing woeful white outfits that made them look like a low-rent magic act. Cole appeared crossing his fingers, no doubt hoping none of his team-mates would ever see the picture of him posing in medallion and 1970s-style suit.

FOOTBALL AT THE MOVIES

Players are accused of play-acting when they hit the deck after the most timid of tackles. Although their theatrical talents are frowned upon in football, they come in very handy when they switch to the silver screen.

Soldier, Soldier

French football has a reputation for producing players with aspirations to act and former Newcastle and Tottenham winger David Ginola joined the ranks in 2004 when he appeared in World War Two actioner *The Last Drop*. Gorgeous Ginola played German soldier Corporal Dieter Max on the hunt for hidden gold and although the film wasn't exactly a huge hit with the critics, the Frenchman's experience of chasing silverware as a player probably came in handy.

Cowboy Cinema

Paul Breitner won the World Cup with West Germany in 1974 but the former Bayern Munich and Real Madrid defender really hit the heights when he appeared in a spaghetti western called *Potato Fritz* two years later. Breitner played the character of Sergeant Stark in the film about a group of Germans in the old American Wild West but despite his best efforts, the acting career never took off and he went back to the day job.

Ally's Alter Ego

A familiar face on the BBC's *Question of Sport*, Rangers legend Ally McCoist swapped the small screen for the big one back in 2000 when he appeared alongside *bone fide* Hollywood heavyweight Robert Duvall in a football drama called *A Shot at Glory*. Luckily for McCoist, it was not the most challenging of roles – he played an over-the-hill, fun-loving striker – although he did deserve some credit for managing not to laugh at Duvall's dreadful Scottish accent in every scene.

Both Barrels

Vinnie Jones enjoyed a reputation as one of football's hardest hardmen in the 1990s, so it was only logical that he'd become a movie muscleman when he tried his hand as an actor. His big break came in 1998 when he landed the part of debt collector Big Chris in *Lock, Stock and Two Smoking Barrels*, a character who finds himself £500,000 (or a week's wages for Cristiano Ronaldo) richer at the end of the film.

Looking For Eric

As a player, Eric Cantona used to 'ghost' into the penalty area on a regular basis and the iconic Frenchman was able to use his spectral skills once again as an actor when he appeared in the 2009 film *Looking for Eric*. Playing a ghostly version of himself, Cantona appears to a football-loving, down-on-his-luck postman to dispense pearls of wisdom about life, family and fate but, sadly, fails to reveal the secrets of the perfect free-kick.

Escape To Victory

The daddy of football flicks, *Escape to Victory* was released in 1981 and tells the story of a group of prisoners of war who, well, escape the clutches of the Nazis after an exhibition match. With football greats, such as Pele, Bobby Moore and Ossie Ardiles, the cast also contained Sylvester Stallone who, legend has it, was so bad at 'playing' a footballer that the director gave the Hollywood muscleman the role of goalkeeper to avoid embarrassment all round.

Stan The Man

Thriller *Basic Instinct* was one of the biggest films of the 1990s but its follow-up *Basic Instinct 2: Risk Addiction* in 2006 was a real flop. Football fans however did at least get to witness the big-screen debut of former Aston Villa and Liverpool striker Stan Collymore, who played the first victim of Sharon Stone's *femme fatale* after an unfortunate and rather rude car crash, proving once and for all that you should keep your hands on the wheel at all times while driving.

Butter Fingers
With the exception of goalkeepers, footballers aren't renowned for their handling skills and Real Madrid's Sergio Ramos proved players are definitely better with their feet than hands when he dropped the Copa del Rey trophy in 2011. Madrid were parading the cup on an open-top bus after beating arch-rivals Barcelona in the final when Ramos lifted it onto his head but let it slip through his fingers, sending the silverware crashing down onto the road and underneath the wheels of the bus following behind.

WE ARE THE CHAMPIONS!

After a long, hard season, winning a trophy is every footballer's dream and once the silverware has been lifted and the champagne opened, the party can really start. Unfortunately though the celebrations do not always go according to plan.

Let There Be Light?
Winning the title at the home of one of your biggest rivals can be a bitter-sweet experience as Portuguese side Porto discovered in 2011 when they beat Benfica at the Estadio da Luz ('The Stadium of Light') to become Primeira Liga champions. As soon as the final whistle sounded, the Porto party began but the celebrations were dramatically cut short when Benfica officials decided to turn off the floodlights inside the stadium and turn on the sprinkler system, leaving the visitors in the dark and drenched.

Touchy Feely
Winning the FA Cup at Wembley is the pinnacle of many players' careers and the emotions of the day surely got to Salomon Kalou in 2012 as Chelsea celebrated beating Liverpool with a team photo with the famous trophy on the pitch. Midfielder Michael Essien proudly held the silverware aloft surrounded by the rest of the Blues team when Kalou suddenly reached up and fondled his team-mate's groin in front of all the cameras, giving both Essien and the assembled photographers much, much more than they'd bargained for.

Smooth Moves

Plenty of players enjoy an impromptu dance on the pitch after winning a trophy but midfielder Kevin-Prince Boateng took things to a whole new level in 2011 after AC Milan were crowned Serie A champions, donning full Michael Jackson costume for the occasion and moonwalking inside the San Siro to 'Billie Jean'. Boateng was cheered along by his Milan team-mates while his agent immediately began negotiations with the Italian version of *Strictly Come Dancing*.

Up In Flames

Temperatures were rising in Brazil in 2009 when Corinthians celebrated winning the Paulista Championship and things suddenly got even hotter when the trophy unexpectedly burst into flames. Covered in tickertape and confetti, the cup lit up when a stray firework ignited the dangling paper, forcing shocked Corinthians players to dive for cover as a desperate scramble for a fire extinguisher followed.

You're Nicked

If there's one way to put a serious dampener on a party, it has to be having your collar felt by the long arm of the law, and that's exactly what happened to hapless Swansea City pair Alan Tate and Lee Trundle as they celebrated the team's victory in the final of the 2006 Football League Trophy. Their crime was to parade around after the final whistle waving a flag with a rather rude message about local rivals Cardiff City – which was really silly considering the final was played in the Welsh capital.

Chest Art

Tattoos are a common way to commemorate a footballing triumph but Wayne Rooney opted for an altogether different kind of body art after Manchester United secured a record-breaking 19th English league title in 2011. Wazza scored the crucial penalty in a 1–1 draw with Blackburn Rovers to confirm United as champions and hours after the final whistle he headed home and shaved '19th' into his chest hair, tweeting pictures of his hairy masterpiece to an unsuspecting world.

In The Night Garden

Winning trophies is child's play for Spain's Fernando Torres. He starred in the Euro 2008 final victory over Germany, scoring the only goal, then played in the 2010 World Cup final victory over Holland. After winning the FA Cup and Champions League with Chelsea in May 2012, Fernando scored and set up a goal in the Euro 2012 final in Kiev against Italy. And he got a special prize for winning the Golden Boot: the right to look after his team-mates' children as they played in the post-match confetti.

Goalkeeper Gaffe

Netherlands goalkeeper Maarten Stekelenburg had a superb 2010–11 season as Ajax were crowned Dutch champions but his normally safe hands spectacularly deserted him on an open-top bus ride through Amsterdam, dropping the trophy as he tried to pass it to team-mate Jan Vertonghen. Fortunately an eagle-eyed policeman picked up the silverware before it was squashed by traffic and handed it to an eager Ajax supporter, who raced after the bus on foot in a desperate but hilarious effort to return the trophy.

Sober Celebrations

When East Fife won the Scottish Third Division title in 2008, it was the club's first silverware for 60 years and surely a great excuse for the mother of all parties. Their celebrations however fell distinctly flat when officers of the Central Scotland Police got wind of the fact the team had the champagne on ice in the dressing room, breaking the law banning alcohol from Scottish sports stadiums, and confiscated the lot.

On My Head, Son

Kicks to the head are an occupational hazard in football but players don't usually expect to get a size nine to the solar plexus after the final whistle has been blown. It happened however to Antonio Cassano in 2012 in the aftermath of AC Milan's goalless draw with Roma, a result which gave the club the Italian title, when he was giving a post-match interview but was violently interrupted by team-mate Zlatan Ibrahimovic karate kicking the side of his face. Whether the pair kissed and made up as the party in the dressing room got into full swing remains a mystery.

Car Trouble

The popping of champagne corks is a familiar sound when footballers have something to celebrate but Bradford City's Stuart McCall opted for a beer or two back in 1999 with disastrous results after the Bantams were promoted to the Premier League. The Scottish midfielder had been knocking back the ale after the club's 3–2 win over Wolves when he joined supporters in the club car park, leaping onto the roof of the nearest motor and then promptly falling off in an embarrassing heap. Unluckily for McCall, his moment of shame was caught on camera.

Morrow Mauled

Ending up in hospital just hours after scoring the winner in a major cup final is far from the ideal way to celebrate victory but it happened to Steve Morrow in 1993 after Arsenal beat Sheffield Wednesday in the League Cup. Morrow found the back of the net in the 68th minute but was denied the chance to party when team-mate Tony Adams picked him up after the final whistle – and then dropped him. The Northern Ireland midfielder broke his arm desperately trying to break his fall and was whisked off to get a cast on the injury in the local A&E, which was definitely not the kind of plastered Morrow had had in mind.

Shirt Shame

If there's one thing guaranteed to annoy fans then it has to be seeing their star player wearing another team's shirt but in the case of Cesc Fabregas in 2010, it really wasn't his fault. Part of the Spanish squad that lifted the World Cup, the Arsenal captain was happily minding his own business as the team celebrated their triumph in South Africa and was powerless to stop Carles Puyol and Gerard Pique forcing a Barcelona shirt over his head. The fact Fabregas actually signed for the Spanish giants 12 months later was absolutely, definitely a coincidence.

CREDITS

The publishers would like to thank the following sources for their kind permission to reproduce the pictures in this book. The page numbers for each of the photographs are listed below, giving the page on which they appear in the book and any location indicator (C-centre, T-top, B-bottom, L-left, R-right).

Action Images: 37TL, 56, 73TL, 142-143; /Roy Beardsworth: 27TR; /Ryan Browne: 13L; /Russell Cheyne/Reuters: 61B; /Leonhard Foeger/Reuters: 2-3; / Richard Heathcote: 91T; /Scott Heavey: 90R; /Mike Hutchings/Reuters: 29TR; /Eddie Keogh/Reuters: 104BL; /Nick Kidd/Sporting Pictures: 16BR; /Michael Kooren/Reuters: 144; /Nicky Loh/Reuters: 85R; /John Marsh: 115TL; /Toby Melville/Reuters: 120C; /Lucy Nicholson/Reuters: 13TL; /Tony O'Brien: 122; / Charles Platiau/Reuters: 151TR; /Carl Recine: 50, 53L, 103BL; /Michael Regan: 80; /Reuters: 23L, 66BR; /John Sibley: 63BR; /Juha Tamminen: 10BL; /Ian Waldie/Reuters: 32B; /Darren Walsh: 21R

Colorsport: 64TR; /Andrew Cowie: 119R; /Stewart Fraser: 73BR; /Ian MacNicol: 8-9

Corbis: /ImageChina: 131BL; /Rainer Jensen/DPA: 134C; /Ben Radford: 1

Getty Images: 5TR, 42; /AFP: 23R, 55TR, 85L, 111BR, 129, 151BR; /Luis Acosta/AFP: 94BR; /Mark Allan/WireImage: 150L; /Vanderlei Almeida/AFP: 57TR; /Odd Andersen/AFP: 88TL; /Keiny Andrade: 81B; /Alexandre Battibugli/ Flickr: 128T; /Sandra Behne/Bongarts: 82L; /Bentley Archive/Popperfoto: 67L, 111TR; /Hamish Blair: 126L; /Pablo Blazquez Dominguez: 138-139; / Shaun Botterill: 5TL, 5LT; /Paula Bronstein: 132-133; /Clive Brunskill: 57BR; / Simon Bruty/Sports Illustrated: 117TR; /David Cannon: 28, 45R, 48L, 149B; / Central Press: 60TL; /Chris Cole: 45BL; /Phil Cole: 95BR, 105BR; /Stephane de Sakutin/AFP: 69C; /Carl de Souza/AFP: 4L; /Adrian Dennis/AFP: 61TR, 121BR; /Kevork Djansezian: 22; /Denis Doyle: 156; /Paul Drinkwater/NBCU: 127TL; /Fred Dufour/AFP: 43R; /Fred Duval/FilmMagic: 153L; /Paul Ellis/AFP: 67T, 145R; /Gianni Ferrari: 57L; /Franck Fife/AFP: 81TR; /Stu Forster: 19; / Gallo Images: 78L; /Lluis Gene/AFP: 55BL; /G Gershoff/WireImage: 149L; / Laurence Griffiths: 11TR, 21TR, 33L, 60B, 96L, 158TL; /Alex Grimm: 114; / Alexander Hassenstein/Bongarts: 82B; /Richard Heathcote: 31TR, 90B; / Patrik Hertzog/AFP: 26; /Mike Hewitt: 18L, 116-117, 119TL; /Samir Hussein: 151L; /Jam Media/LatinContent: 39TL; /Geoff Holmes/AFP: 86BL; /Jasper Juinen: 13BR, 145B; /Henryk T Kaiser: 84B; /Glyn Kirk/AFP: 92-93; /Pornchai Kittiwongsakul/AFP: 128B; /Olaf Kraak/AFP: 79L; /LatinContent: 100B; / Christopher Lee: 53R; /Alex Livesey: 15L, 70-71, 83R, 97TL, 115BR; /Thomas Lohnes/AFP: 120-121; /Philippe Lopez/AFP: 74L; /John MacDougall/AFP: 33TR, 105C; /Stuart MacFarlane/Arsenal FC: 105L; /Hannes Magerstaedt: 47BL;

/Clive Mason: 95L; /Jamie McDonald: 34-35, 123TR; /Buda Mendes/ LatinContent: 109B; /Vesa Moilanen/AFP: 124-125; /Filippo Monteforte/AFP: 158L; /Don Morley: 55BR; /NTI: 109R; /Kazuhiro Nogi/AFP: 130TR; /Mustafa Ozer/AFP: 135TL; /John Peters/Man Utd FC: 12L, 39BR; /Matthew Peters/Man Utd FC: 30L, 67R, 157B; /Joern Pollex/Bongarts: 25BL, 58-59; /Popperfoto: 4BC, 5RT, 20-21, 45TL, 46B, 54TR, 99BR; /Andrew Powell/Liverpool FC: 87TL; /Savo Prelevic/AFP: 16L; /Gary M Prior: 71TR; /Miguel Queimadelos Alonso: 101L; /Cristina Quicler/AFP: 123BR; /Ben Radford: 49L, 49B; /Miguel Riopa/ AFP: 159BL; /Quinn Rooney: 51TR; /Martin Rose/Bongarts: 103TR, 111L; / Roberto Schmidt/AFP: 62BR; /Marc Serota: 5RB; /Roberto Serra: 100R; / ShowBizIreland: 147; /Janek Skarsynsky/AFP: 117R; /Javier Soriano/AFP: 146TL; /Ben Stansall/AFP: 137R; /Thomas Starke/Bongarts: 89; /Michael Steele: 11B, 75R; /Patrik Stollarz/AFP: 70L; /Bob Thomas: 7BC, 7BR, 27TL, 32TR, 39L, 48L, 49BR, 63TL, 64B, 69TR, 78R, 78BR, 79R, 94TL, 101T, 106-107, 109TL, 135BR, 143TL, 160; /Brendon Thorne: 44C; /Topical Press Agency: 131BR; /Omar Torres/AFP: 38; /Anton Uzunov/AFP: 95T; /VI Images: 110; / Eric Vandeville/Gamma: 131TR; /Claudio Villa: 20R, 99TL; /Thorsten Wagner/ Bongarts: 37TR; /Todd Warshaw: 49TR; /Hiroki Watanabe: 52R; /Anders Wiklund/AFP: 75TL; /Chris Wilkins/AFP: 65TR; /Andrew Yates/AFP: 10T, 18T, 88L, 96R; /Laurent Zabulon/Gamma: 62L; /Vittorio Zunino Celotto: 146BR

Mirrorpix: 5LB, 24, 25TR, 25R, 102; /Peter Cook: 33BR; /Albert Cooper: 7BL; /Monte Fresco: 30-31, 148TL; /Brendan Monks: 14

Offside Sports Photography: /Steve Bardens: 5BL, 108; /Mahe Bertrand/ L'Equipe: 41TR; /Charlie Crowhurst: 118T; /L'Equipe: 66L; /Mark Leech: 15R, 51TL, 82TR, 85TR, 116R, 159T; /Simon Stacpoole: 91R; /Witters: 72R

The Picture Desk: /Kobal Collection: 154R

Press Association Images: 4BL, 97BR, 141TR; /AP: 11L; /All Action: 83T; / Matthew Ashton: 69B, 115BL; /Jake Badger/Landov: 76-77; /Peter Byrne: 37BL; /Eamonn and James Clarke: 142TL; /Barry Coombs: 44B; /DPA: 134TL; / David Davies: 5BR; /Adam Davy: 84T; /Sean Dempsey: 104TR; /Mike Egerton: 101BR; /Nigel French: 98; /Anna Gowthorpe: 36; /Ross Kinnaird: 27BL; /Claire MacKintosh: 105TR; /Tony Marshall: 5C; /Andrew Milligan: 12B; /Phil Noble: 72L; /Julio Pantoja/AP: 148R; /Andrew Parsons: 145TR; /Gabriel Piko: 51B; / Sergey Ponomarev/AP: 65B; /Duncan Raban: 153TC; /Martin Rickett: 100TL; / Peter Robinson: 54BL, 68, 118BR; /S&G and Barratts: 4BR, 86-87, 112-113; / Michael Steele: 17BR; /Studio Buzzi: 157TR; /Alessandra Tarantino/AP: 61L; / Vincent van Doornick: 52L; /John Walton: 123C; /Aubrey Washington: 57BC; / Ian West: 136L

Rex Features: 6, 40; /Albanpix: 127B; /BackPageImages: 29BR; /Ted Blackbrow/Daily Mail: 17T; /Peter Brooker: 43L; /Mark Campbell: 46TL; /Andre Csillag: 149TR; /Everett Collection: 154BL, 155T, 155BL; /Fremantle Media: 41TL; /Harry Goodwin: 150BR; /Rupert Hartley: 7C; /Robin Jones: 140; / MGM/Everett Collection: 155R; /Mercury Press Agency: 47R; /NTI: 130BL; / Quirky China News: 136-137; /F Sierakowski: 153TR; /Sipa Press: 41L; /Martin Stenning: 141BR

Topfoto: 88BR; /ActionPlus: 74BR; /National News: 152

Every effort has been made to acknowledge correctly and contact the source and/or copyright holder of each picture and Carlton Books Limited apologises for any unintentional errors or omissions that will be corrected in future editions of this book.

Paul Gascoigne sets out to prove that he could have run rings around Ruud Gullit and Diego Maradona in their prime.